the more you think something needs to be fixed
the more you need to let it go!

Releasing
RESISTANCE

what you're attracting ←

38 HIGHLY EFFECTIVE WAYS TO CHANGE
LET GO the little things holding you back
and LET IN the big things you really want

Elizabeth Richardson

What's Inside This Book?

Who is this book for? 6

How long does it take for things to manifest? 6

How will this book benefit me? 8

Who's the author of this book? 10

Advice for "A Happy" Life 17

Monitoring Your Progress 21

My Story 27

EMPOWERING PROCESS # 1 To Give Myself Permission 29

EMPOWERING PROCESS # 2 To Reveal Silent but Deadly Beliefs ... 35

EMPOWERING PROCESS # 3 To Treat Myself Well 37

EMPOWERING PROCESS # 4 To Get My Inner Beings' Perspective. 41

EMPOWERING PROCESS # 5 To Align with Source 43

EMPOWERING PROCESS # 6 To Keep Moving Forward 45

EMPOWERING PROCESS # 7 To Have More Fun 47

EMPOWERING PROCESS # 8 To Receive Clear Answers 49

EMPOWERING PROCESS # 9 To Bring Me Back into Alignment 51

EMPOWERING PROCESS #10 To Comfortably Give and Receive 55

EMPOWERING PROCESS #11 To Attract More Money 57

EMPOWERING PROCESS #12 To Move Forward Rapidly 61

EMPOWERING PROCESS #13 To Make Things Happen Quicker 63

EMPOWERING PROCESS #14 To Find Peace 75

EMPOWERING PROCESS #15 To Sleep Well 77

EMPOWERING PROCESS #16 To Overcome Addictions 79

The Spiritual 12 Step Program 83

EMPOWERING PROCESS #17 To Change an Old Habit................... 87

EMPOWERING PROCESS #18 To Guarantee Instant Success......... 89

EMPOWERING PROCESS #19 To Get Organised............................ 91

EMPOWERING PROCESS #20 To Feel Better About Anything......... 93

EMPOWERING PROCESS #21 To Be an Influence in The World 99

EMPOWERING PROCESS #22 To Love Myself More 101

EMPOWERING PROCESS #23 To Change My Attitude.................. 103

EMPOWERING PROCESS #24 To Help Anyone Feel Better........... 107

EMPOWERING PROCESS #25 To Reclaim My Power.................... 109

EMPOWERING PROCESS #26 To Make My Dreams Come True.... 113

EMPOWERING PROCESS #27 To Calm Down............................... 115

EMPOWERING PROCESS #28 To Make Better Choices 117

EMPOWERING PROCESS #29 To Start My Day Off Well 119

EMPOWERING PROCESS #30 To Transform A Relationship 121

EMPOWERING PROCESS #31 To Move On From A Relationship .. 123

EMPOWERING PROCESS #32 To Start All Over Again 125

EMPOWERING PROCESS #33 To Catch Up with My Dreams......... 127

EMPOWERING PROCESS #34 To Get Back To Centre Quickly....... 129

EMPOWERING PROCESS #35 To Thank The Universe.................. 133

EMPOWERING PROCESS #36 To Release Resistance.................. 135

EMPOWERING PROCESS #37 To Be A Conscious Creator 137

EMPOWERING PROCESS #38 To Let Go And Trust The Process .. 139

Checking Your Progress... 141

Thank You.. 143

Contact Details 145

Who is this book for?

Releasing Resistance is for men and women who generally know what they need to do, but just can't seem to do it!

If any area of your life feels stagnant, stale, or stuck, whether it be in a relationship, the lack of relationship, money, health, home, work, your body or your business, you will be given the tools to help you get momentum flowing in a positive direction, steadily, increasing in intensity, while gently raising your vibration.

This book not only helps you find out exactly what's been holding you back but gives you a systematic way so you can effectively, easily and sustainable LET GO those pesky little resistant things once and for all and LET IN the big things you really want to manifest instead!

How long does it take for things to manifest?

As long as it takes for you to RELEASE THE RESISTANCE!

"When people ask us how long does it take for something to manifest, we say, "It takes as long as it takes you to release the RESISTANCE. Could be 30 years, could be 40 years, could be 50 years, could be a week. Could be tomorrow afternoon." - Abraham-Hicks™

How will this book benefit me?

This book contains proven and highly effective processes to release resistance, so that you can find relief, peace, contentment and joy more often, more consistently and more sustainably, without some other person or life condition needing to change.

It also contains leading edge answers to some very common questions.

- What to do when you want to have better relationships.
- What to do when you need to overcome addictions.
- What to do when you don't have enough money.
- What to do when you are desperate to lose weight.
- What to do when you haven't been able to get what you want.
- What to do when you need to release the resistance.
- What to do when you doubt your abilities.
- What to do when you keep procrastinating.
- What to do when you think you're too old, too ugly, too tired, too stupid or too broken etc.

Most times we think that it takes BIG changes to improve our lives, when really it's the little everyday habits that hold us back the most. Silent self-criticism, getting up in a rush, worrying about things that may never happen, doing work out of obligation instead of joy, eating things we know aren't good for us, watching the news, telling people what's gone wrong instead of celebrating what's going right, feeding our fears, doubting our own capabilities, getting upset about world events that we can't possible change ... what this book does is make changing ourselves easy! With this series of simple but powerful processes, the change happens inside us, which then manifests in the world around us. It helps us feel more purposeful, more aligned, more determined, more empowered and more confident to go out and truly live the lives, we secretly dream of living.

Improving your life starts with modifying the most simple, everyday thought patterns that we're giving energy to, often without realizing. It works like a light dimmer switch. If you switch the light from fully-on to fully-off, you notice the difference immediately. But a small negative thought practiced occasionally, just dims your life force over time. But it will get your attention eventually. By then, you will notice it through outer physical manifestations, like health issues, decreased energy, tiredness, accidents, relationship challenges, work dissatisfaction, emotional instability, mood swings, unhappiness, addictions and drama.

The empowering processes contained in this book, while often simple, quick and easy to fulfill, hold a high potential for positive personal expansion. The concepts you are about to practice, require a slight shift in focus, conversation and habitual action in order to create the space to receive the things you would prefer to manifest in your life instead. Sometimes the biggest shift occurs when we realize we've been working way too hard to get what we want, and all it takes now is to let go the struggle, release the resistance and allow it to be easy.

Expect to receive those shifts, in your awareness, belief system, identity, habits, emotions and most importantly, in your results. The recommendation is to set a time of about 17 days to complete all the processes, and to get the most benefit.

I'm truly looking forward to hearing about what's worked for you and how you may have modified any of the processes to suit your individual situation.

What feels right for you matters,

Elizabeth Richardson

https://elizabethrichardson.info/contact

Who's the author of this book?

Hi, I'm Elizabeth, author, and passionate advocate of tapping into *Flow States* as often as possible. I like knowing what I write, helps others experience more peace, satisfaction, self-love, and positive expectation.

Every living being emits a unique vibrational frequency. I believe how we vibrate is the key to health, wealth, happiness, and success. When your vibe is high and you feel good, everything flows effortlessly; but when your inner world is unsettled, facing challenges in the outer world becomes significantly more difficult. My goal is to uplift—so you feel *more* ease, and *less* stress.

With a rich background as a professional counsellor, group therapy leader, and well-being advocate, I've had the privilege of training with some notable experts like Robert Kiyosaki (Rich Dad Poor Dad) and Tony Robbins, continuously integrating self-development into my professional journey. I am also a certified Conscious Breathing Practitioner (Australian Institute of Rebirthing).

As the author, or co-author of over 15 Feel Good books, I manage to seamlessly blend personal fulfillment into every aspect of my work. My life and business philosophies are deeply inspired by the teachings of Abraham-Hicks™. These days I thoroughly enjoy my freedom to contribute where I feel most valued and inspired. My passion for living, loving, and laughing, remains at the forefront of my focus.

How can I get the most out of this book?

There are five attitudes what will prevent any change from happening in an instant. Let's handle those upfront:

1. I already know this stuff!
2. I don't understand!
3. I don't agree with that!
4. I've done these sorts of things before!
5. It won't work for me!

"Whether you think you can or think you can't - you're right!" - Henry Ford

If you've found yourself thinking any of those things – stop! Open your mind, suspend judgment for a while and allow yourself to get benefit from these next two simple steps before deciding to do anything else.

❖ STEP 1: LISTEN TO THE "YOU" INSIDE OF YOU FOR A MOMENT.
How are you feeling right now?
Have you picked up this book in a rush? Are you just skimming through to see if it will grab your attention, or are you relaxed and ready to really enjoy the possibilities of what's about to unfold?
What is the YOU inside of you saying?
What would that part of you like to do right now?
What would happen if you DID that?

So much resistance is created because we're doing what we think we "should" instead of doing what we really want. Often we listen to others so much, we've dulled our own ability to hear, feel, see and know what our own inner guidance is calling us to do.

❖ STEP 2: MAKE PEACE WITH WHERE YOU ARE
Let wherever you are in your life right now, be OK.
Because, it IS OK.
You are where you are and it's the perfect place to start.

Relax your shoulders, relax your spine, relax your mind and relax your body a little.

Take a couple deep breaths and let them go easily, gently, peacefully, fully.

Feel the relief in doing that.

Congratulate yourself.

Say, "Well done!"

You've just released a chunk of resistance. So now, if you're ready and if you really want to, settle into a comfortable position with this book, grab a notepad, a pen, a drink of water and let's begin.

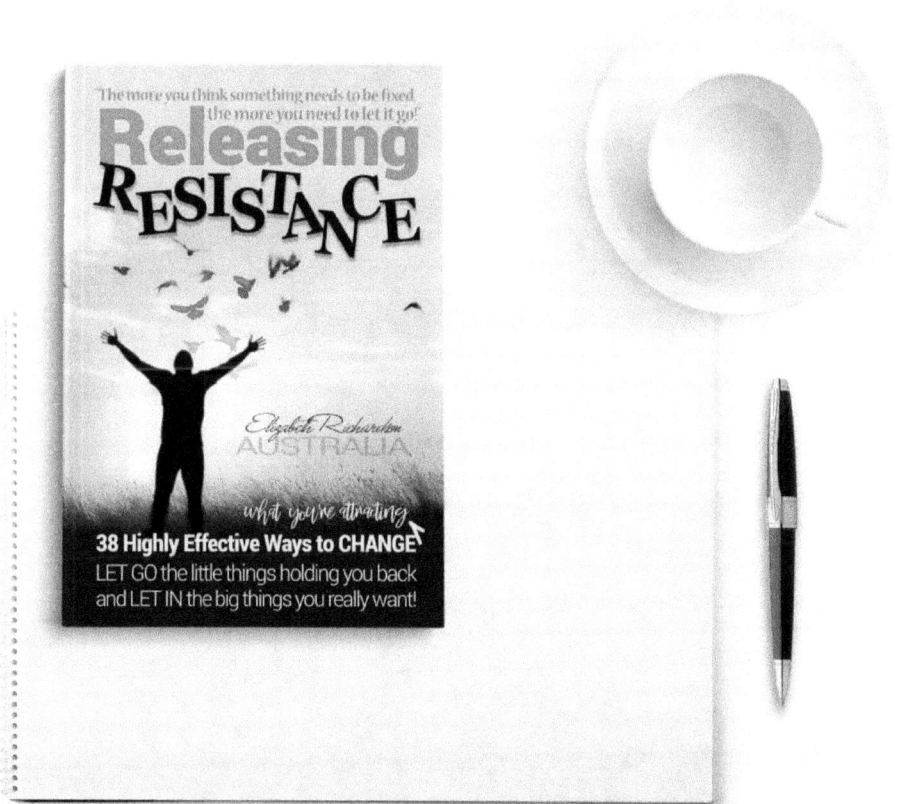

Introduction

"Happiness is Natural"

It's NOT something we need to work at, it's NOT something that's just gifted to the rich and famous, it's NOT something that only happens when we get the things we think we want, it's something that we can RELAX INTO, whether we've got enough money to pay our bills, whether we've found the love of our life, whether we're enjoying our work, whether the right people are running the country, whether we've found the cure for whatever is ailing us, whether we're living in the house of our dreams, whether we're as fit, healthy, smart or slim as we think we should be, or not!

But how can I be happy when things are the way they are?

"Happiness happens, when you release resistance!"

By definition, resistance means:

1. The refusal to accept or comply with something; the attempt to prevent something by action or argument:
   "they put up no resistance to being shown a different way"

2. The degree to which a substance or device opposes the passage of an electric current, causing energy dissipation.
   "the old wires were causing enough resistance to significantly reduce the steady flow of the current".

Throughout our lives we're exposed to thoughts from other people around us, from influencers in society like TV, Movies, publications, product manufacturers and social media and, from evaluating our own experiences. Thought itself, is a process of asking and answering questions.

If we were able to just receive a thought and let the ones we don't like pass by, life would run smoothly, but when something happens, good or bad, as humans we ask ourselves: "What does this mean?"

The answer *we've made up* to make sense of the question, "What does this mean?" does one of three things:

1. It empowers us to move forward and thrive.
2. It passes by, leaving little or no residue.
3. It creates resistance by keeping us stuck at the point of impact.

When I started to become more aware of the answers I was making up inside my mind about all sorts of things; I laughed. Life changed rapidly for me from that moment on.

I even found myself thinking; "When something good happens – that means I'm good!" So, when something bad happens - does that mean I'm bad, or wrong or flawed in some way?

"We make life mean whatever we want it to mean!"

So, let's start to make these things mean something that gives us POWER to adapt, to change, to move, to improve, to energize, to contribute, to excel, to open, to grow, to expand and to truly thrive.

Advice for "A Happy" Life

Each one of the suggestions you are about to read are an empowering process in themselves. They help to form a foundation for the work (or play) we'll be doing together throughout the course of this book. I like to call them *Advice for Life*.

You might like to pick the ones that mean the most to you and write them down in your notepad. Read them each day for the next 17 days to remind you of the little things that can release your resistance to receiving whatever it is you still want to be, do, have or create in your life.

1. DECIDE TO FEEL GOOD: Everything we want is because we think it will make us feel better once we get it. Decide that feeling good is the most important thing to you. Write it down and put it somewhere prominent for the next 17 days and remind yourself often. "Feeling GOOD is the most important thing to ME!"

2. SPEAK WELL: Speak only good things about yourself and others. If you can't say something genuinely nice, if you can't say something kind to yourself, if you can't say something supportive of others, don't say anything at all. Don't beat yourself up or criticize another person, your mate, your kids, your boss, or the Government. Just let it go as if it didn't happen. Yes. You CAN do this!

3. GET READY: Imagine that you are about to expand in the most wonderful ways and prepare yourself, your body, your home, your cupboards, your mind, your life, to receive it. Make it fun.

4. LIFT YOUR SPIRITS: Do ONE thing every day to raise your vibration. Find something new, interesting, relaxing or fun to do for 5 to 10 minutes every day; something that gives you tingles, lights up your life or makes you shine (maybe walking in nature, singing, dancing, watching inspirational videos, playing a musical instrument etc.) Stay away from the media altogether if you can during this time. The difference this can make, might shock you.

5. BELIEVE IN YOURSELF: Stop second guessing your past decisions, actions, dreams or what's possible to create in the future. You don't need to prove anything to anyone, especially to God. You were born worthy. You are important. You are valued. You are loved. Trust and affirm, "I can have it, just because I want it!" You might want to write that one down too.

6. SAY "THANK YOU" MORE OFTEN: Find something to thank someone else for, daily. Find something to thank the Universe for, daily. Find something to thank yourself for, as often as you possibly can. Start now!

7. DREAM BIG: Visualize having an absolutely wonderful life and that it could happen in a myriad of different ways. Feel what it would feel like. DON'T do this for more than a few minutes at a time. The purpose is to feel and practice the vibration of the end result – not to plan the steps to getting there or to question how it will happen. Visualize it while it feels good then change focus. Dart in and dart out. Practice the same thing with conversations. Do it while it feels good, then move on to something else.

8. FIND THE BENEFIT: No matter what's happening, what someone is saying, what actions you've taken in the past, what course you're doing or what book you're reading right now, even if there's something you don't like, don't yet understand or don't agree with – look for the benefits.

9. FOLLOW THROUGH: Make a commitment every day to something small and stick to it. You might feel inspired to make a commitment to completing the processes in this book, or to just reading it all the way to the end. Its simplicity and potential is life changing. When you live with integrity (integrity with yourself, not how someone else thinks you should be), you feel stronger, more confident, sure of who you are and what you have to offer the world, and you'll be much more empowered in all other areas of your life too.

10. PAY ATTENTION TO HOW YOU FEEL: Notice every time you feel good, make a fist in the air and say "Yes" out loud or raise both hands up high and activate an alpha state.

11. PRACTICE ALLOWING: Release resistance in any way you can by quietening your mind if it's chatting negatively. Don't expect to stop negative momentum in full flight though. Just slow it down as best you can by taking some breaths and letting the energy pass. And it will pass. When you notice the resistance lift and you start to feel better, that's the time to celebrate. That's the time to say your affirmations. That's the time to write. That's the time to share your story. That's the time to close that business deal. That's the time to make love. That's the time to DO whatever your bliss is calling you to do. The energy that flows freely during this time, creatively achieves much more than at any other.

12. BE BOLD: Stop playing safe, being cautious or worrying about what could go wrong! You will never regret making a mistake that brings you further clarity about what you want like you will regret not having thrown everything into living fully while you have the chance. Live life to the max, one small step at a time.

13. MAKE DECISIONS FROM A HIGHER VIBE: Decisions made in anger or resentment exacerbates downward spiralling momentum. Line up your energy to be as close to genuine satisfaction, and appreciation as you can BEFORE making any major decisions. While no decision is ever wrong, the decisions we make from an empowered state tend to take us rocketing into the future with ease, positive momentum and great passion.

14. ACT ON INSPIRATION: Take action from inspiration - not desperation - not obligation - not frustration. If you've been procrastinating, don't beat yourself up. Take it easy. It just means the inspiration wasn't strong enough or you hadn't lined up your energy properly first. Some people will feel inspired to take action after the first day of reading this book, others, later on. But just know, if you follow these easy exercises, the inspiration for whatever is right for you will surely come, and you will know exactly what to do next.

15. BE TRUE TO YOU: Only YOU know what's right for you. You know when something feels good, when it resonates, when it's easy, when it just flows, and you also know when something about it feels *off* in that moment. If you want to do something - do it. If you don't – let it go!

If you read this list every day for the next 17 days, it will start to sink in how happy, free, and joyful these simple principles will make you feel. Write down the insights you receive along the way.

Monitoring Your Progress

LET'S DO A QUICK CHECK TO FIND OUT WHERE YOU ARE RIGHT NOW.

On a scale of 1 – 10 (with 10 being the highest, the best, the greatest) write down the answer to each of these next questions.

How relaxed and at ease am I feeling right now about:

1. My health.
2. My physical body.
3. My finances, sense of freedom and money.
4. My family and relationships.
5. My work, career or business.
6. My home, location and environment.
7. My contentment and satisfaction with the life I'm currently living.
8. My ability to be, do have and create more of what I want in the future.
9. My connection to Spirit/Source/God/Higher Self?

THEN SET A TANGIBLE INTENTION FOR WHAT YOU'D LIKE TO RECEIVE BY READING THIS BOOK.

I Intend to Be, Do, Have, Feel or Create:

....

LETTING GO THE RESISTANCE: If there's something you've been working on (health, relationship, money, career, weight-loss, success, beauty, fame or anything else) for more than 90 days and it still hasn't manifested in your life, then for the next 17 days, don't talk about it, don't think about it, don't take any unnecessary action towards it, don't activate anything about it at all. (If you've listed it as your intention in the step above, it would be a really good idea to replace it with something else – for now!)

The purpose here is to let go the resistance to receiving it FIRST.

This is a friendly and abundant Universe. Law of Attraction reflects back to us what our dominant vibration has been. There is only one reason why things you really want haven't yet manifested, and that is because you keep activating the opposite of what you do want, by creating resistance, with a conflicting belief.

Over the next 17 days, these beliefs will soften naturally. You don't have to find and change them; you don't have to go to a counsellor to get rid of them and you don't have to visit a life coach to illuminate them. These simple processes will help them dissipate in the easiest, fun and most sustainable way possible. You will simply forget they were even there.

SIDE NOTE: Back in the early 90's I spent 2 years in close relationship with a World Class Hypnotherapist and Neuro Linguistic Programmer. One of his clients, a Company Executive, came to him to get rid of his "Fear of Flying" as his work now demanded that he travel on a regular basis. Robert ran into him unexpectedly at the airport a few years later and said, so it seems you got over your fear of flying, and the man said, "What fear of flying?"

Sometimes we are so good as practitioners, that our clients forget there was even a problem.

Parenting is a bit like that too. We often give enormous amounts of time, patience, and love to our children and sometimes we are acknowledged for it, sometimes we are not. There aren't accolades and awards for some of the best work we will do in the world - that's why it's important, to do everything because it makes YOU feel good in the moment. Reaching out a hand of support, offering words of encouragement, paying a genuine compliment, even just walking down the street with a smile can have a bigger impact on our own lives and on the world around us, much more than we'll ever know.

Did you set a tangible intention for what you'd like to receive from reading this book in the step above? If you weren't inspired to do that, perhaps you'd like to do this instead.

SET A SILLY GOAL ... & CHOOSE A NEW IDENTITY TO MATCH IT

HERE'S A REAL-LIFE EXAMPLE: When I decided I was ready to have a new, fun, happy and deliciously loving relationship, I changed my way of setting a goal, went out to the forest feeling child-like, whimsical and a little crazy, and asked the fairies to give me a handsome prince, a white horse, and a carriage.

The new identity I chose for myself: I AM the Queen.

THE RESULT: My mate and I started talking only a few days after that. It was truly magical.

What's your silly goal?

....

....

....

What would you need to let go if this was to come true?

....

....

....

Who would you need to become?

I AM .... (your new identity)

LIFE CIRCUMSTANCES DON'T CHANGE INSTANTLY, although sometimes it might seem like they can. Just as a change of weather is preceded by a change in barometric pressure, a change in circumstances is always preceded by a change in your emotional and vibrational state.

The intention of this book is not to solve your problems, but to raise your awareness and your vibration so your problems solve themselves. The higher our vibrational state, the higher quality our newly inspired thoughts, ideas, words, decisions, actions, and opportunities will be.

The greatest resource we have is our ability and desire to achieve a more empowered emotional state and practice it until it becomes our dominant experience. Reading though this book and doing the processes will naturally open your mind, expand your consciousness, and uplift your spirits, and when you feel better emotionally, you'll feel more in control of your life. It's counterproductive to try and control outer circumstances in an attempt to feel good. Changing our energy changes everything!

Are you ready for more? We've set some new energy in motion. Let's keep moving.

DISCLAIMER: This information is intended to be used for personal development and entertainment purposes. Any consciousness shifting processes you undertake may be accompanied by feelings that are a little different or uncomfortable at times, as you are changing beliefs, attitudes, and vibration at a core level. Define for yourself what feels different and what feels *off*. This is meant to be light-hearted, interesting, empowering and fun. That *different* feeling is called expansion. Your consciousness is being expanded. I like to say, "*My Life is expanding and I'm going with it*" which helps me relax and go with the flow of one of the most natural processes of all, growth. If we don't grow — we die. The feelings of expansion are most often described as butterflies in the stomach, excitement, feeling weak at the knees, gut instinct, fluttering in the chest, and you may even experience an "*opening of the heart*" (especially during and after deep meditations).

EMPOWERING RECOMMENDATION: Do your best to complete the activities when you feel pretty good or while remaining in alignment. If an activity, process or recommendation does or doesn't feel right for you, TRUST your own guidance.

"Do not try to fix the problem, instead, find alignment. Let your alignment bring the solution!" - Abraham-Hicks™

My Story

For me, writing is a side-effect. Powerful words, super-creative websites and all sorts of cool designs are inspired through me as a result of Releasing My Own Resistance on whatever topic currently has me in its grasp. You see, when I have a problem that's caused sleepless nights, an accident, illness, or lethargy, not wanting to work, failing to eat properly, or go for my regular walks along the water that I generally love with a passion; I always know what I need to do.

Start meditating again!

Why is it that we often know what we need to do, but we just don't do it, we can't find the time to do it or it feels like something is preventing us from doing it consistently or even doing at all?

It's called resistance! And the more you try and push yourself, the more you go into silent self-criticism, berating yourself for putting things off, being lazy or even worse, telling yourself you're a failure --- and the stronger it gets, the deeper you dig yourself into the muck.

If this has happened to you, you are NOT alone!

For me personally, I know that a breathing meditation first thing in the morning is one of the biggest *Power Moves* I can ever make.

Meditating not only Releases the Resistance that's been keeping me stuck, but after doing it for a while, it rockets me into the next phase of my life, with greater awareness, more compassion, a deeper understanding of what other people go through and strong, strong, strong desire to live fully, laugh whole-heartedly and love completely yet again. The next thing I know, that problem I thought I had, has virtually disappeared. I've moved around it, recovered from it, overcome it, got over it, or ignored it long enough, that it fixed itself!

But for 6 months of last year, I was so out of whack, that trying to meditate, was driving me crazy! The thoughts I didn't want to think were getting louder, the emotional and physical pain was unbearable, I became reclusive, only going out at night to get food (because I didn't want anyone to see me in the light of day), I was totally unable to contribute anything of value to others and the problems seemed to be compounding one on top of the other, to the point that I was questioning whether my life was even worth living. To get relief from the craziness, I had to stop and take time out from everyone else and from ALL personal development and self-improvement work entirely.

I lay on the couch day and night for months, barely moving, recovering from a physical injury that made it painful to get up, my two cats kept me sane, providing entertainment and giving me a reason to live - for the moment. I started watching TV (something I had rarely done for about 12 years now). With a complimentary subscription to Foxtel, I caught every episode of whatever Home Improvement Shows were available, sometimes watching up to 20 hours straight. I was too embarrassed to tell anyone about the state I was in, until much later.

Throughout my life I've been extremely successful in various fields --- I never thought in my wildest dreams, I'd end up like THIS! Inside I knew, that staying still was the best option for me, so I GAVE MYSELF PERMISSION (EMPOWERING PROCESS #1) to take as long as I needed doing absolutely "*nothing useful*" until "*something*" shifted. I reminded myself nothing stays the same forever --- and this too would change! One way or another.

EMPOWERING PROCESS # 1
To Give Myself Permission

INTRODUCTION: This process has been written specifically to help you think outside the box and raise your vibration. It's particularly useful if you've got yourself in a double bind, where you're damned if you do something and damned if you don't.

INSTRUCTIONS: Adapt the empowering statements suggested next to suit your own situation. They are intended to help you feel better and to release any resistance to the changes you are currently asking to receive.

Pick the ones that feel soothing as you read them. Pick the ones that move energy in you. Pick the ones that bring a sense of relief, freedom, lightness or liberation. It might benefit YOU to write them down in your notepad and read them to yourself over the next 17 days, and sign it with your own name too.

For the moment, don't judge them as good or bad, right or wrong. If it makes you feel a little better for now, then it's serving its purpose!

May your journey be easier because of them.

With so much love,

Elizabeth Richardson

Statements Designed to Release Resistance

I give myself permission to BE DEPRESSED BECAUSE OF this relationship, this problem, this hardship, this turmoil, this family, this job, this situation, this home, this country, this world.

I give myself permission to BE SAD ABOUT this relationship, this problem, this hardship, this turmoil, this family, this job, this situation, this home, this country, this world.

I give myself permission to BE ANGRY ABOUT this relationship, this problem, this hardship, this turmoil, this family, this job, this situation, this home, this country, this world.

I give myself permission to WANT REVENGE BECAUSE OF this relationship, this problem, this hardship, this turmoil, this family, this job, this situation, this home, this country, this world.

I give myself permission to FEEL HELPLESS ABOUT this relationship, this problem, this hardship, this turmoil, this family, this job, this situation, this home, this country, this world.

I give myself permission to FEEL GUILTY ABOUT this relationship, this problem, this hardship, this turmoil, this family, this job, this situation, this home, this country, this world.

I give myself permission to BLAME SOMEONE ELSE FOR this relationship, this problem, this hardship, this turmoil, this family, this job, this situation, this home, this country, this world.

I give myself permission to BE BORED WITH this relationship, this problem, this hardship, this turmoil, this family, this job, this situation, this home, this country, this world.

I give myself permission to FEEL HOPEFUL ABOUT this relationship, this problem, this hardship, this turmoil, this family, this job, this situation, this home, this country, this world.

I give myself permission to BE RIGHT ABOUT this relationship, this problem, this hardship, this turmoil, this family, this job, this situation, this home, this country, this world.

I give myself permission to BE WRONG ABOUT this relationship, this problem, this hardship, this turmoil, this family, this job, this situation, this home, this country, this world.

I give myself permission to LET GO OF this relationship, this problem, this hardship, this turmoil, this family, this job, this situation, this home, this country, this world.

I give myself permission to HOLD ON TO this relationship, this problem, this hardship, this turmoil, this family, this job, this situation, this home, this country, this world.

I give myself permission to FORGET ABOUT this relationship, this problem, this hardship, this turmoil, this family, this job, this situation, this home, this country, this world.

I give myself permission to FREE MYSELF FROM this relationship, this problem, this hardship, this turmoil, this family, this job, this situation, this home, this country, this world.

I give myself permission to RESOLVE this relationship, this problem, this hardship, this turmoil, this family, this job, this situation, this home, this country, this world.

I give myself permission to WANT SOMETHING BETTER THAN this relationship, this problem, this hardship, this turmoil, this family, this job, this situation, this home, this country, this world.

I give myself permission to TRANSFORM this relationship, this problem, this hardship, this turmoil, this family, this job, this situation, this home, this country, this world.

I give myself permission to NOT UNDERSTAND HOW I ATTRACTED this relationship, this problem, this hardship, this turmoil, this family, this job, this situation, this home, this country, this world.

I give myself permission to FORGIVE MYSELF FOR ATTRACTING this relationship, this problem, this hardship, this turmoil, this family, this job, this situation, this home, this country, this world.

I give myself permission to TAKE RESPONSIBILITY FOR this relationship, this problem, this hardship, this turmoil, this family, this job, this situation, this home, this country, this world.

I give myself permission to RELEASE MY SENSE OF OBLIGATION TO this relationship, this problem, this hardship, this turmoil, this family, this job, this situation, this home, this country, this world.

I give myself permission to GET BENEFIT FROM this relationship, this problem, this hardship, this turmoil, this family, this job, this situation, this home, this country, this world.

I give myself permission to FEEL BAD ABOUT this relationship, this problem, this hardship, this turmoil, this family, this job, this situation, this home, this country, this world.

I give myself permission to FEEL BETTER ABOUT this relationship, this problem, this hardship, this turmoil, this family, this job, this situation, this home, this country, this world.

I give myself permission to BE THANKFUL FOR this relationship, this problem, this hardship, this turmoil, this family, this job, this situation, this home, this country, this world.

I give myself permission to FIND PEACE IN this relationship, this problem, this hardship, this turmoil, this family, this job, this situation, this home, this country, this world.

I give myself permission to LEAVE this relationship, this problem, this hardship, this turmoil, this family, this job, this situation, this home, this country, this world.

I give myself permission to KEEP this relationship, this problem, this hardship, this turmoil, this family, this job, this situation, this home, this country, this world.

I give myself permission to RELEASE this relationship, this problem, this hardship, this turmoil, this family, this job, this situation, this home, this country, this world.

I give myself permission to ALLOW this relationship, this problem, this hardship, this turmoil, this family, this job, this situation, this home, this country, this world.

I give myself permission to CHANGE this relationship, this problem, this hardship, this turmoil, this family, this job, this situation, this home, this country, this world.

I give myself permission to BLESS this relationship, this problem, this hardship, this turmoil, this family, this job, this situation, this home, this country, this world.

I give myself permission to BE PASSIONATE ABOUT this relationship, this problem, this hardship, this turmoil, this family, this job, this situation, this home, this country, this world.

I give myself permission to FEEL EMPOWERED BY this relationship, this problem, this hardship, this turmoil, this family, this job, this situation, this home, this country, this world.

I give myself permission to GET VALUE FROM this relationship, this problem, this hardship, this turmoil, this family, this job, this situation, this home, this country, this world.

I give myself permission to ADD VALUE TO this relationship, this problem, this hardship, this turmoil, this family, this job, this situation, this home, this country, this world.

I give myself permission to ADORE this relationship, this problem, this hardship, this turmoil, this family, this job, this situation, this home, this country, this world.

I give myself permission to LOVE this relationship, this problem, this hardship, this turmoil, this family, this job, this situation, this home, this country, this world.

I give myself permission to APPRECIATE this relationship, this problem, this hardship, this turmoil, this family, this job, this situation, this home, this country, this world.

You have permission ....

I give you permission ....

We grant you permission ....

God gives you permission ....

"I give myself permission to BE HAPPY, to find peace, to get relief in any way I can, to feel liberated, to live in luxury, to enjoy comfort, to work with passion, to go for the things I truly want, to take time out whenever I need it, and to love with all my heart." – ER

EMPOWERING PROCESS # 2
To Reveal Silent but Deadly Beliefs

*"Identify your problems
but give your power and energy to solutions."*
Tony Robbins

Beliefs are such funny things. They aren't true. They aren't real. They aren't even accurate. They're just thoughts we keep repeating to ourselves (and sometimes to others) that can sit in the back of our minds and continue to attract repeated results in our life, often without our conscious awareness. This simple process will reveal a set of blocks unique to each one of us, so they can be changed instantly to what we prefer them to be instead. Be spontaneous when you answer so you more easily access the deepest truth, not the practiced mind games.

HERE'S THE GAME: Speed write a list of reasons why you're not as successful as you'd like to be. Then write what is really true.

I'm not as successful as I'd like to be because:

....

....

What's really true is:

....

....

....

....

....

When I first did this process, I was also inspired to list evidence that proved the old belief was bogus, while affirming the new conscious belief that I wanted to keep repeating instead.

Don't think too much about it. Don't dwell on it. Do the process and if you're inspired to expand it like I was, do whatever feels right for you --- and then let it go. The purpose is to become "*aware of the resistant thoughts*". The best processes are very, very simple, and very, very powerful.

Shouldn't I know all this stuff already?

You do know this stuff. I'm just reminding you in perhaps a slightly different way than you've experienced before, and if there are questions you've been wanting the Universe to answer for you, if there are problems you've been trying to solve, if there are issues you've wanted to get clarity around ... and you are here now, then it's right where you're meant to be. Open yourself to receive.

EMPOWERING PROCESS # 3
To Treat Myself Well

"Discipline is only a short-term deterrent. It has never been responsible for long term change – only encouragement, upliftment and love can possibly do that!" – ER

❖ Do you ever say, "That was a stupid thing to do!"?

❖ Do you ever look in the mirror and feel dissatisfied with what you see?

❖ Do you ever compare yourself unfavourably to others and assume you're not as good as they are?

❖ Do you ever declare, "There must be something wrong with me!"?

❖ Do you ever wonder why you haven't got your life handled by now?

❖ Do you ever tell yourself you shouldn't do something, like eat the food you love, or drink too much, or be too lazy?

❖ Do you ever think, "If only I was thinner, fitter, richer, smarter, healthier, happier, younger, funnier, wiser ... ?

Self-criticism is never valuable, productive, or constructive. Self-criticism creates the most resistance of all. If you don't believe me and you've been telling yourself how bad you are in an attempt to change something about yourself ...
well, how's that working out for you?

A GAME FOR LIFE: Every time you catch yourself being self-critical, find three things you genuinely like about yourself and talk about those instead.

MY STORY: During a stressful period in my life, I put on quite a bit of weight. When I'd get up in the mornings and look in the mirror, I kept being reminded of how unhappy I was in my relationship, how my life was going downhill and how dissatisfied I was with the state I'd let my body get in. One day after I started meditating, I got up, walked past the mirror again, cringed, then realized how destructive I was being to the person I'm meant to love the most. I allowed myself to think the dreaded thought briefly, *"Oh, God, I'm fat!"* Then I decided, *"But you know what, I'm sexy!"* and I started to dance like some of the most confident erotic dancers I'd ever seen, loving my beautiful breasts, my shapely curves, my smooth skin, my long, luscious hair ... life was never the same again!

A while back, Facebook was prompting responses to the question *"What are your most notable achievements?"* My response was easy. I'm 10 kilograms lighter than I was this time last year; not because I worked at it, but because I changed my *attitude* about it. And once I decided what my new attitude would be, the rest was easy, and liberating, and quick, and fun, and exciting, and most of all, it was thoroughly empowering.

Here's how my attitude once shaped my body.

- ❖ Whenever I decided I needed to *"lose weight"* –
  I ended up putting on more weight.
- ❖ Whenever I got annoyed with my *"lack of willpower"* –
  I reached for comfort food to console myself.
- ❖ Whenever I had the thought *"I'll be happy if I just get thinner!"* –
  I got more and more unhappy.

❖ Whenever I looked in the mirror *"dissatisfied with what I saw"* —
  I saw more imperfections, not just in my body but with my home,
  my relationship, my wardrobe, my life.

Can you see a pattern?

Here's how I changed my attitude and got better/instant results.

❖ If I caught myself thinking about losing weight —
  I decided to think about *"how I want to feel"* so much more.
❖ If I started to put myself down for being slack —
  I chose to *"acknowledge the things I'm actually doing well"* instead.
❖ If I looked in the mirror and began to criticize myself —
  I looked for lots more things to *"compliment myself on"* too.
❖ If I thought about being happy sometime in the future —
  I declared *"I'm gonna find something to be happy about right now!"*

Within 3 days, my whole life began to shift. I started being drawn into
taking actions that perpetuated health and vitality and fitness and
outdoors and movement and aliveness and freedom and fun. I didn't
push myself. I didn't need to set concrete goals. Everything I did was
because I loved doing it. I did work that I thoroughly enjoyed too, and
it was EASY, because of one thing and one thing only …

… I started being nicer to ME.

"LOVING MY SELF …
Acknowledging who I've been,
valuing who I am,
adoring who I'm becoming." – ER

"LOVING MY JOURNEY …
Accepting where I've been,
appreciating where I am,
celebrating where I'm going." – ER

~ Notes ~

EMPOWERING PROCESS # 4
To Get My Inner Beings' Perspective

INTRODUCTION: Instead of being hard on yourself, would you like to find out what your Inner Being thinks of you instead?

If you've been criticizing yourself for a long time, this next process might be a bit annoying, upsetting, confronting, boring OR exhilarating, depending on how open you are in the moment to receive. It's great to do it with another person and we often do it in Self Development Workshops to help get large numbers of people in a room to be totally present. If you have pets, you probably do it with them already, without even noticing.

So that we don't have to rely on anyone else, you can also do this process with yourself. 10 minutes is usually as much time as it takes. If it's a struggle, let it go, maybe you'll get more benefit from doing it another time; however, it is one of the most powerful and simple processes for change that I know.

HERE'S THE PROCESS: Look deeply into your own eyes in the bathroom mirror, until you can hear or feel distinctly, what your Inner Being REALLY thinks about you.

"Now I'm loving myself so much more." – ER

EMPOWERING PROCESS # 5
To Align with Source

Here's a simple process to activate positive energy on topics such as Prosperity, Health, Career, Money, Love and Relationships.

THIS IS THE GAME: With pen and paper, physically write these words as often and as many times as you feel inspired. It's OK if it gets monotonous and repetitive. Just imagine all the repetitive crap that's probably been running around in your head now being replaced with something so much more life enhancing. FEEL the uplifting energy of these words as you write them too. Pure magic!

Love Appreciation Freedom Fun Joy Clarity Energy Passion Power

~ Notes ~

EMPOWERING PROCESS # 6
To Keep Moving Forward

Late last year, I was inspired to create and release a new program. My Facebook page was humming, the stuff I wrote publicly was getting lots of attention, people were showing up out of the blue, the research I'd done showed me it had the potential to be extremely successful and this aspect of my life was getting exciting, flowing smoothly and gaining momentum.

Then I noticed a day when the energy backed off a little, there were less *likes* to my daily Facebook posts and I wondered what was "*going wrong*". Each morning when I woke up, I immediately turned on my phone and checked to see how many *likes* I'd been given overnight. I started to be more critical about what I was posting. I even deleted some posts and rewrote others. I tried posting stuff that had been really successful before but got disappointing results. I frantically kept checking for positive responses multiple times throughout the day, and questioned myself, doubted myself, worried myself silly.

Can you see what I was doing?

I was taking score, based on what other people were or were not doing. I was looking for validation outside myself instead of allowing the inspiration to keep flowing from inside me. I was looking at what HAD happened, instead of looking forward to where I was being called to go.

Do you have a little habit like that too? A habit that you think is so insignificant that it can't be too bad. That little habit is most likely creating *big resistance*!

Don't take score too soon. Don't keep checking for proof that something is working. Don't look for faults and flaws and problems. Don't second-guess yourself. Those things will most likely throw you out of your happy-place, and being happy is what creates the ideal atmosphere for the rest of those wonderful things you want, to come easily to you.

A GAME FOR LIFE: When you become aware of the funny little habits you've picked up that create resistance --- LAUGH! Decide to let them go for the next 17 days, then look ahead at what you'd rather do instead. Letting go might take some practice because of the momentum that funny little habit has, but the more you look ahead and enjoy what you're in the process of creating, the easier it is to change.

"You don't need to focus on growth at all. Put all your emphasis on joy. People are getting frustrated wanting to accomplish what they think is in their Vortex. `Let the Vortex do the accomplishing. Just focus on the Joy."
– Abraham-Hicks™

EMPOWERING PROCESS # 7
To Have More Fun

Let this day be about fun. Looking for, generating, activating, talking about, thinking about, writing about, allowing as many opportunities for fun to present themselves as you possibly can. But if fun is a little elusive today, don't feel bad about it; just soothe yourself into taking life a little bit lighter than you probably have been.

"The day I spontaneously decided to do this process, I had one of the most fun days ever; and got paid for it!" – ER

~ Notes ~

EMPOWERING PROCESS # 8
To Receive Clear Answers

"When I raised the quality of the questions I asked myself, it dramatically improved the quality of my life as well." – ER

Most of us seem to have a repetitive question that we ask ourselves unconsciously, especially when something goes wrong. Often this question is disempowering in nature as it's something we picked up in the early years of our life based on how others thought we should behave. My disempowering question once was, *"Oh God, what have I done wrong now?"*

When I started asking the *"right"* questions, I found the answers I really wanted to hear; answers that were uplifting, answers that moved energy in me and answers that rapidly propelled me forward, to the life of my dreams.

HERE'S THE PROCESS: Remember when something awful happened? Can you think of a disempowering question you asked yourself at that time? Maybe it's something your parents asked you when they were in a bad mood. Maybe it's something a teacher would say on a bad day. We all think and say things we don't mean when we're out of our happy-place, so let go any blame. Find the old question and replace it with a better quality one and empower yourself to make a conscious change. Write down the new question in your notebook so it's easier to remember. I don't need to tell you to be more aware of these disempowering questions from now on, because your Inner Being is on the case already.

EMPOWERING QUESTIONS TO ASK YOURSELF INSTEAD:

- What do I really want now?
- What's the potential benefit here?
- What does my Inner Being think about this?
- What would "*love*" do now?
- What good might come out of this?
- What has worked out for me?
- What gets me excited about life?
- What's right about this?
- What positive things happened today?
- What can I find to be happy about now?

Ask yourself those questions and answer them as often as you can. Drop the need to ask, "How WILL something happen?" That's not your work. It's the work of God/Spirit/Universe to show us the way.

My new questions are:

....

....

....

....

....

EMPOWERING PROCESS # 9
To Bring Me Back into Alignment

THE PROCESS: Develop an Empowering Affirmation or Incantation.

When I'm fully open to inspiration, the words that flow through me often rhyme. The following Mantra came when I was in the middle of writing 500 Confessions. It's easy to remember AND most importantly, it isn't just some affirmation that I repeat mindlessly, it actually moves energy when I speak it! It soothes, it comforts, it brings me more into the present moment, and the present moment is where all my power is. I find this one particularly useful when I'm going through some sort of emotional turmoil.

Incantation to Bring Peaceful Relief:

I am where I am and it's the perfect place to start.
I have what I have and it's more than enough.
I'm creating what I'm creating by what I think, say and do.
I'm going where I'm going, and a thousand angels are
with me too.

Anthony Robbins (Life and Business Strategist, Philanthropist, Entrepreneur and #1 New York Times Best Selling Author), spends a significant amount of time prior to any event, speaking engagement or meeting, defining, choosing and intending the way he wishes to feel. It's called, *getting into an empowered state*, *getting in the zone* or *getting aligned*. One of the techniques he uses is to repeat certain key sentences in a particular way to deliberately produce a more heightened sense of wellbeing. These positively affirming statements, when combined with feeling, energy, movement, and emotion, are called "*incantations*". I'll include some of his that are appropriate for several different situations here, and if you've ever been to one of his Programs, you'll be very familiar with the first one.

Incantation to Lift Your Emotional State:

I am the voice.
Now "I" am the voice.
I will lead not follow,
I will believe, not doubt,
I will create, not destroy.
I am a force for good.
"I" AM a LEADER.
Step up!
Step UP!
STEP UP!

Incantation to Stimulate a Feeling of Abundance:

Gods' wealth is circulating in my life.
Gods' wealth FLOWS to me in avalanches of abundance.
All my needs, desires and goals are met instantaneously
by infinite intelligence, where I am one with God and
God is everything.

Getting back into alignment isn't just about being high and happy all the time. Emotions aren't meant to be static. The word emotion even means "*energy in motion*". Every time you feel resistance lift, your energy is moving back into closer alignment with your Source, God, Inner Being, Spirit or Higher Self (whatever you like to call it), so simply feeling a sense of relief is heading in the direction you want.

Acknowledge yourself for being able to move energy consciously. For most of us, it takes practice and it's a skill well worth cultivating.

QUESTION: Do you have some words that help move energy in you too?

If not, use any of these, change them to suit your own magnificent uniqueness, ask to be inspired to write OR sing OR rap some of your own, when you're ready to receive them.

....

....

....

....

....

....

....

....

....

....

~ Notes ~

EMPOWERING PROCESS #10
To Comfortably Give and Receive

PART 1: This is a useful little game to play in a group setting or around the family dinner table, where you encourage each person to contribute the answer to the following two questions. Children of all ages respond really well to being asked important questions like these, especially if we let them speak freely without interrupting or trying to improve their answers.

Don't put too much thought into it or you'll say something you've already been practicing that's most likely causing resistance. Perhaps you'd like to wait until you're *really in the zone* and let the answers be more inspired, but if you're ready to go, answer spontaneously now.

Say the first thing that comes into your mind.

1. *Name one thing you have to contribute to the world?*

2. *Name one thing that you would you like to receive from the Universe?*

PART 2: GIVE UNCONDITIONALLY … Do things because they make you feel good, not because you feel obligated, not because someone said you should, not because you think others can't do it for themselves and not because you expect something in return.

MOST IMPORTANTLY, GIVE UNCONDITIONALLY TO YOURSELF FIRST … then let the excess shower over others. When you're overflowing with love you have an abundance to give. Do it for joy, have fun and most of all, because you can. Give time, give talent, give love, give happiness, give compliments, give a smile, give a helping hand.

BE OPEN TO RECEIVE … No one on this entire planet ever needs to prove their value. We were ALL born worthy.

The Great Spirit gave us life,
a sun that rises every day,
birds that sing happily,
children forever calling us to play.

A perfect heart that keeps beating,
without giving a second of thought.
The rain, the seasons, the mountains,
none of us ever went out and bought.

When you settle into these concepts,
a bigger picture can be seen.
There's so much more to this life
than most of us dare to dream.

Let your inner guidance lead you,
choose feelings you want to experience now.
There are not many things more enjoyable,
than to relax, ask once … and ALLOW! – ER

EMPOWERING PROCESS #11
To Attract More Money

"I love money and money loves me!"

I remember when I was training myself to have a more prosperous attitude. I knew I had to make some changes if I wanted the quality of my life to improve. My attitude sure needed some adjustment, and when I became conscious of some old thoughts I'd picked up along the way and replaced them with prosperity enhancing ones, the results were fantastic.

When bills came in and I didn't know how I was going to pay them ...

- ❖ the tendency was to look for ways to get bigger discounts,
- ❖ the tendency was to get involved in insane conversations about the rising cost of living or about how expensive things were,
- ❖ the tendency was to say I couldn't do or have something because I couldn't afford it,
- ❖ the tendency was to react with a sense of dread when I thought about the money I owed, to feel bad, to worry and reduce my ability to get creative,
- ❖ the tendency was to feel ashamed when I couldn't pay for dinner.
- ❖ the tendency was to be a bit annoyed that other people I knew didn't seem to be struggling, the same way I was,
- ❖ the tendency was to criticise how my neighbours, my friends, the government or big corporations were spending their money too.

But I decided to develop a new tendency ...

- ❖ I decided that when bills came in instead of DOUBTING I could pay them, I just WONDERED what might happen.
- ❖ I decided that when I paid for something I'd consciously declare, *"There's plenty more where that came from!"*
- ❖ I decided to give up the need to get discounts, to look for bargains and to shop in cheap stores.
- ❖ I decided to remember how resourceful I really can be.
- ❖ I decided to be more trusting in the power of my own alignment to naturally draw more good stuff to me.
- ❖ I decided to do simple things that I loved, that felt good and that made ME feel special and prosperous and free.
- ❖ I decided to be more accepting about how I was feeling.
- ❖ I decided to stop listening to the crowd.
- ❖ I decided to mind my OWN business.
- ❖ I decided to celebrate and keep even the smallest coins I found on the street.
- ❖ I decided to allow ideas, opportunities, and creativity to flow.

Then I watched my world shift to match my new decisions ...

- ❖ I spent so much less money because I was filling myself up with happiness, not with objects,
- ❖ People started giving me money or helped me out for no reason, other than they simply wanted to,
- ❖ Incredible, ridiculously priced bargains for things I'd often dreamed of, showed up seemingly out of the blue,
- ❖ I wasn't charged for electricity for 12 months because of a mistake the power company made,
- ❖ Clients even to this day put money in my account without me even billing them,
- ❖ Cash appears on the ground in front of me, in shopping centres, on the footpath, in the mail, in clothes or bags I haven't used for some time,

- ❖ My passive income became more regular, from more different sources, and increased out of sight,
- ❖ Ideas for exciting future projects started to flow,
- ❖ I was inspired to write like never before, in the middle of the night, in the middle of a date (that was funny), in the middle of conversations. Words flowed with a clarity, ease and insight that often surprised even me.
- ❖ When I see something that I want, I just let myself want it – PERIOD, and if I still want in in time to come, the ways and means are always provided.

HAVING A RICH LIFE WASN'T SOMETHING THAT HAPPENED BECAUSE I WORKED HARD … (though when I'm inspired I can work effortlessly and joyfully for 20 hours straight and still want to do more), it didn't happen because I got lucky (though I feel phenomenally blessed), it didn't happen because I made the right investments (though the most incredible opportunities just keep finding me) and it didn't happen because I followed some brand new internet marketing scheme or developed a master finance plan. My plan is to have fun, to be happy, to follow my bliss and to trust I'm being guided every step of the way.

PROSPERITY IS AN INNER JOURNEY FIRST … When I gently trained my mind to recall more abundance stories, when I deliberately started conversations about how wonderful life can be and when I stopped comparing myself to others, life slowly started to feel better … and everything else is history.

"NOW I LOVE GETTING BILLS …
It means I have the ability to pay them." – ER

"I LOVE PAYING MY BILLS TOO …
It means that prosperity is flowing in and out, in and out,
in and out, like the air that I breathe." – ER

HERE'S YOUR TASK IF YOU CHOOSE TO ACCEPT IT: Grab your notebook. Write down what your past tendency has been towards money, and write down what you could change it to instead, just like I did. Then get creative about how your world might shift because of this change in attitude. Let your imagination run wild. Notice if you're receiving any new thoughts that you've never thought before. If that happens – CELEBRATE. Yay! You're in the receiving mode. That's all you needed to do.

....

....

....

....

....

....

....

....

EMPOWERING PROCESS #12
To Move Forward Rapidly

While it's beneficial to notice where our resistance lies and make changes so we can attract more of the things we really want, the best way of all to move forward rapidly, is contained in this awesome game below.

A GAME FOR LIFE: When things are going well, CELEBRATE, GENERATE, CULTIVATE, SALIVATE and APPRECIATE. Keep the empowered energy moving and expand it as much as you can.

"Leave resistance behind forever,
by making the good things ever better!"

~ Notes ~

EMPOWERING PROCESS #13
To Make Things Happen Quicker

How can I build up momentum so the things I want come quicker?

HERE'S THE ANSWER: Procrastinate occasionally! Yes you heard it. Procrastinate occasionally, and quit chastising yourself for those times you haven't taken action!

How often have you started something and not finished it? That hasn't happened because you're flawed in some way, that's because there wasn't enough positive energy moving on the topic to begin with.

If you listen to most people, it's easy to assume that procrastination is a bad thing. Even the dictionary definition includes words like, "delaying tactics" "stalling" and "playing a waiting game".

The worst part is the way we criticize ourselves when we fail to take action on a task that we decide, should have been done, would be better if it was done or really needs to be done.

Self-criticism is never a positive motivator and if done regularly, tends to have debilitating effects on our self-esteem, health and general well-being. Self-criticism produces negative emotions such as guilt and shame, and any action taken from a lower vibration like that is naturally setting us up for failure.

This next section will change your attitude about what you (or others) have been doing. It will let go lots of resistance and raise your vibration. It also includes its own "*7 Step Process*" that has the potential to improve your life forever!

Just reading the introduction will most likely release resistance with or without your conscious awareness. It answers the most common questions people have when faced with being told that procrastinating is not a dirty word after all, and you'll be given rational and logical explanations for how it can actually benefit you.

INTRODUCTION:

Why do we procrastinate?

Over the years, I've experienced two distinct types of procrastination:

1. Putting things off that I wanted to, or needed to get done.
2. Starting things and not completing them.

Being critical of myself for putting things off, initially led me to think there was something wrong with me. So I decided to push myself harder and start things that I had no energy or inspiration to finish, which led to even worse results.

There were times when I started something because I thought I "*should*" do it, I felt "*obligated*" to do it or other people "*recommended*" I do it, not because I actually "*wanted*" to do it, felt inspired to do it or really enjoyed doing it.

If you're like me, you might have also developed a "*need*" for conditions to be perfect before you decided to write that book, clean out that cupboard, leave that job, improve that relationship, give away that stuff, pursue that career, start that business, buy that yacht, create that new product, follow that dream …

The pursuit of perfection is an avoidance tool that stops us getting anything done, and, is completely unnecessary. The continuation of life is about progress, growth, evolution and expansion - not perfection!

The truth is, there is no perfect time or perfect way to do anything; however, there are times when we can line up our energy, thoughts and beliefs so purely and powerfully in a *"positive"* direction, that the right action, producing brilliant results, are virtually unstoppable.

And if you have ever taken action when you're in a "negative" spiral, like in a fit of anger, rage, fear or insecurity, you will remember how quickly things spun out of control and, that those actions are the ones you later regretted the most.

This spiralling energy is called momentum.

It isn't right or wrong, it's just the way energy works. If you give something attention when you're feeling good, it produces positive results. If you give something attention when you're feeling bad, it produces negative results. And the more attention we give anything, the more speed it gains.

Why does momentum matter?

When we decide that there's something we want to be, do, have or create in our lives, we start energy flowing towards that desire. If we keep following that desire WITHOUT introducing thoughts that contradict it, the energy flows faster creating momentum, like a snowball rolling down a hill gathering speed and extra mass as it goes. As the momentum increases, the ensuing passion fuels it to fruition. That sounds pretty easy doesn't it!

What's stopping me getting the things I want easily?

Contradictory thoughts will do that. When you start to introduce the odd thought of doubt, worry, insecurity, fear, concern or uncertainty about being able to have what you want, the energy splits and flows in the opposing direction as well. Here's a common example of positive and negative energy at work on the same topic:

- ❖ I want it but I don't think I can get it.
- ❖ I want it but I don't know how it's going to happen.
- ❖ I want it but nobody else I know has done it.
- ❖ I want it but I'm not good enough, smart enough, rich enough, thin enough, experienced enough … … … well, you get the gist!

From this example, you can imagine how the energy is oscillating from one side to the other. This stalls our progress forward, produces more conflicting beliefs and puts us in a stalemate.

But guess what? It turns out, that procrastination is an action (or inaction) based on great wisdom!

Read on to find out why!

> *"Procrastination is the wisdom to not try and force something that you're not vibrationally ready for." Abraham-Hicks™*

Well, that leading edge quote certainly made me change my mind, and guess what? If you really let it sink in, you've probably just changed your mind too and turned procrastination into a potential benefit, which releases your resistance to receiving things you put pressure on yourself to do in the past and you'll be much more open to receive the juicy pieces of information coming on the following pages.

Realizations happen, in the right place, at the right time, according to the emotional vibration we are emitting.

Our task isn't to try to fix problems, but to change our vibration and then allow the solutions to come to us. So all congratulations go to you for being ready, open and willing, to receive.

But I've been stalling. I must have some conflicting beliefs. What can I do about those?

Don't try and push through it — go out and have some fun. Stabilize into an easy vibe or get momentum flowing in a positive direction on some other topic — any topic will do.

But shouldn't I try and change these conflicting beliefs instead?

You can try. But why work so hard by tackling it head-on when you can go about it indirectly and have much more fun?

To change anything, we don't need to change the condition, we can instead, change our vibration, and the condition will eventually match the energy that we're putting out to the world - OR - new and improved conditions will be drawn to us.

So go out, relax, change your focus and come back to this when your energy is fresh, because if you feel inspired to do the next "*7 Steps*" they will move you once and for all, away from split energy, inaction, self-criticism and doubt, into gentle acceptance, openness and change for the better.

The following 7 Steps are simple, at times confronting, and powerful, and work best if your energy is light, happy, positive and eager. You may like to allow the good part of an hour to let this entire process work its magic.

Get ready to receive!

"Don't try and talk yourself out of wanting something because you haven't figured out how to get it yet. You want to drive fast. Don't slow down - just remove the trees!"
Abraham-Hicks™

~ 7 Steps ~

to

Move Positively Forward
Towards the Life of Your Dreams

Do you think you deserve better than what you've been getting?

Would you like to know what to do from now on, to help you *naturally* move energy more purely towards the life of your dreams?

Completing these simple but profound 7 Steps, will empower you to change behaviour that was once misunderstood and bring clarity to your future journey – guaranteed!

Grab a pen and paper. Physically putting things in writing adds further power to the process. Making a gentle commitment to completing it right now, adds even more.

STEP 1. WHAT DO YOU REALLY WANT?

Getting clear about what you really want gives you power. Power gives you the impetus to act. Most people don't get what they want because they aren't clear about what they want.

They've never defined it in ways that truly shifts energy and creates momentum.

Saying that you want money or a relationship or to lose weight or to give up smoking just doesn't cut it anymore. And, if you've been asking for something for more than 90 days and it still hasn't come, then it's time to shake things up a bit. It's time to ask in a slightly different way.

- ❖ What do you REALLY want? In your heart, in your soul, not what society, TV, your parents or other people tell you. What do you REALLY want today, right now, in this moment?
- ❖ Write all of the things you want on a piece of paper, and then choose ONE of those topics. Choosing ONE little thing to focus on now, is better than not doing a lot of big things!
- ❖ If right now you had that one thing, how would it make you feel?
- ❖ Feel what that feels like for a minute or two, and then move on to the next question.

STEP 2. WHY DO YOU WANT IT?

Talking about, *"what you want and why you want something"* is an empowering process in itself. If you take this step alone and do it for a few minutes every day, after 72 hours you will notice a positive shift in your energy. You may even be noticing it right now.

BUT HERE'S THE KEY: Do it when it feels good to do it – not because you want to make something happen!

All of life responds to vibration. It responds to how you're really feeling inside, not to what you say on the outside, and if you have a hidden agenda, if you're trying to manipulate the Universe into giving you something that you aren't vibrationally ready to receive, then you are thwarting your own intention.

So, decide to do it simply because it feels good – for now!

I want .... because ....

Explore the reasons why you want it even more. Use as many different modes to explore these reasons as you can, like speaking, thinking, singing, listening, watching and writing them. Why do I suggest this? Some people are more visual and respond best by seeing. Some people are more auditory and respond best by hearing. Some of us are more kinaesthetic and respond by feel, touch, body position and movement. Here are some great examples of answering these questions using different modes:

❖ THINK about what you want and why you want it as you hold your hand on your heart;
❖ WRITE about it in as much detail as possible then read it back to yourself while standing with a straight posture, holding the piece of paper in your hands at eye level and keeping your head up;
❖ LISTEN to yourself talking about it by making a recording on your phone and playing it back through ear plugs while walking, exercising, doing the housework or dancing;
❖ SPEAK it or SING it out loud in the bathroom mirror. Keep your eyes open and notice the response on your face;
❖ WATCH yourself talking about it by making a quick video, taking note to see if you look convinced that you can have it, and if not, perhaps you'd like to shoot another video that's a little more convincing;
❖ HAVE FUN WITH IT, jump up and down as you talk about what you want and why you want it, punch your fist in the air and yell "YES" as you list each reason.
❖ ACTIVATE the energy of it in whatever ways work best for you until you feel a positive shift ---- then answer the next question!

STEP 3. WHY DON'T YOU ALREADY HAVE IT?

Here's where a significant piece of resistance lies! The answer to this question is often the missing link to success! It's usually laced with excuses, blame and justifications.

If you truly want to know what's been holding you back — it's you — it's always you! Don't berate yourself. Simple becoming aware of these reasons is enough to shift energy.

Relax and trust the process.

Write down all the reasons why you "think" you don't already have it.

I don't have it yet because:

....

....

STEP 4. DECIDE TO TAKE A SIMPLE FIRST ACTION

Well done! Awareness is powerful. Now that you're more aware of the thoughts, beliefs or attitudes that have been holding you back, decide on a single, specific first action towards what you want. Decide to do something that's new, something that you're not in the habit of doing, something different, or something that will be pretty easy or fun to complete.

It may encompass your body, mind and spirit — but it doesn't matter — make it simple so that it gains some momentum — make it something that is so simple you'll wonder if it's worth doing — and make it something you'll actually do within 24 hours.

STEP 5. MAKE A COMMITMENT

Commitment is one of the secrets to success. But commitment is often a misunderstood concept. A commitment like this is made to yourself. It is about you. It is for you. Don't make the commitment because I told you to do it. Do it because and if, it feels right for you.

Right now, you want to set yourself up for easy success – thinking about, writing about, talking about and committing to completing this 7 Step Process was a good place to start. Committing to taking the simple first action you decided on in Step 4, is a good one too.

Keeping your commitments to yourself, means you are living with integrity. Not someone elses' version of integrity – just your version of integrity – and it moves energy and speeds up momentum tenfold.

But the commitment shouldn't feel heavy; it should just feel do-able, interesting, possible and achievable and maybe even a little exciting. Remember, that doing ONE little thing now, is better than not doing a lot of big things!

STEP 6. REWARD YOURSELF

Positive reinforcement is powerful. Reward the behaviour you want. We are changing habits here so this step is vital to the continuation of more supportive and effortless actions. And it's also great fun!

Punishment has never been a long term deterrent, only love and acceptance can bring about sustainable change. One of the best ways to practice an improved vibration is to CELEBRATE when things are going well (but be very quiet when they're not).

What will you give yourself if you complete this action within 24 hours?

If you actually give yourself the reward you decide on in this step, you will add to the positive momentum, you will keep taking positive steps forward and long-term change is inevitable.

STEP 7. BE ACCOUNTABLE

If you could have achieved this on your own, you already would have! So in this step I am suggesting that you make yourself accountable to someone else. Tell them a little about what you're doing and why you're doing it. No need to make it a major conversation, just do it in passing.

That's it.

Completing this simple step flows energy just that little bit faster again. Doing this process in simple step form just as it's been set out, allows momentum to build gradually and manageably.

Perhaps you remember a time when energy moved really fast towards something you wanted, and it started to feel overwhelming! Freaking out, stops it completely. Focusing on something else for a while that is relaxing and rejuvenating in nature, slows it down enough so you can manage it better when your vibration stabilizes again.

The Universe likes speed, and you will too. These 7 Steps help get momentum moving on one topic that is important to you, in ways that create conscious awareness, release resistance, focus you incrementally forward, feel good, connect you more fully to your own spirit and make actual sense.

Well done! Take the rest of the day off!

EMPOWERING PROCESS #14
To Find Peace

THE PROCESS: Meditate on one word or short phrase throughout the day that bring a sense of settled balance to your life when you say them. Simple words or phrases such as Thank You, Welcome, I Surrender, "I'm Right and You're Right" and "Things are always working out for me", can often bring instant relief.

They don't have the potential reaction factor that words like Love, God, Money and Health tend to stimulate because these ones are usually related to conditions. For example, I love you when you're good to me. God Loves me when I do His will. Money and Health are good if I have them.

Thank You, Welcome, I Surrender, "I'm Right and You're Right" and "Things are always working out for me", don't require any conditions to be fulfilled to be able to say them, really mean them and, for them to settle our emotional state and restore equilibrium.

This is a particularly useful exercise during trauma, stress, emotional turmoil or ongoing conflict to slow down negative momentum long enough to change the direction of the vibrational flow. No one ever needs to suffer.

"Pain is part of life. Suffering is optional."
Tony Robbins

*What words
bring a sense of peace and calm
when YOU say them?*

EMPOWERING PROCESS #15
To Sleep Well

HOW TO SLEEP IN PEACE - WAKE UP AND SHINE!

What do you tend to do after you get home from a big day out?

Some people might have a glass of wine with dinner, play a mind-numbing video game, take a warm bath, exercise, watch something action-packed on TV, draw in a few deep breaths on a cigarette, read a good book, eat some chocolate, light a scented candle, masturbate, meditate in silence or relax their bodies and minds in a myriad of other ways.

Everything serves its purpose. Most habits are created to soothe us, to take us away from stress, to get us to think about something else or to take us away from our worries, even if it might not be considered health, relationship or life enhancing by society, by our family or by our mate.

Your body and mind both need a chance to settle after the energy rush many people experience throughout their days. Most of us are good at slowing our bodies down, but what about our minds?

How often do you go to bed trying to solve problems that you faced during the day or worrying about what might happen tomorrow?

HERE'S A NEW GAME TO PLAY INSTEAD: A few moments before sleep, release any thoughts that take you away from being fully present in the moment by using the *"resistance releasing"* process I'm about to give you. But just telling you to release thoughts rarely works. To successfully let go one thing, you need to hold on to something else. The magic happens by drawing your focus away from your worries and giving your mind a task that is simple enough to do without creating stress, gentle enough without stimulating angst, yet focused enough to keep you on a straight and easy track.

Think of a few positively uplifting words beginning with a particular letter of the alphabet and feel the energy of them as you list them, like ...

C = contentment, comfort, connection, closeness, calm, certainty, clarity, cuddle, cheerful, complete, creative, colourful, celebrate, crystal, cash, caress, comfortable, confident, content, curious ...

A = amazing, appreciation, anticipation, alive, awesome, amazed, attractive, animated, aware, abundance, alignment, adventure, attraction, awareness, absolutely, accepting, admiration, affectionate, assured, affinity ...

E = enthusiastic, eager, encouraging, ease, ecstatic, enhancing, exhilaration, exciting, energy, enchanting, exuberant, energetic, engrossed, expansion, essence, effervescent, evolving, extravagant, everlasting, extraordinary, exceptional, elated ...

> *"Don't underestimate the power of this simple game. Focusing on ANYTHING that raises our vibration naturally lifts us into a better emotional state and attracts improvement in all areas of life." – ER*

EMPOWERING PROCESS #16
To Overcome Addictions

Here is a simple technique that helps you discover more about yourself ... and usually uplifts you too. Often the revelations can be both enlightening and really funny, so be open to the answers that come to mind as you start to write. If you are reluctant to do this publicly, then at least give it a go in private, but there is nothing like a newly inspired, honest, simple high-vibe process as a catalyst to begin to make a change.

Firstly let's see how society defines if you have an addiction:

❖ You keep thinking about (your addiction) and anticipate the next time you will be indulging in it.
❖ You need to keep using (your addiction) more often to feel satisfied.
❖ You have tried unsuccessfully to control or stop (your addiction).
❖ You feel moody, upset or angry when you try to control or stop (your addiction).
❖ You regularly indulge in (your addiction) longer or more often than you originally intended.
❖ You have severely compromised or risked the loss of a significant relationship or career opportunity because of (your addiction).
❖ You have lied to people close to you to conceal the extent of (your addiction).
❖ You use (your addiction) as a way to escape from your problems.

❖ You suffer some type of physical, mental or emotional problem as a result of (your addiction).

Using A Notepad, Answer These Four Questions

1. *What benefits does the addiction "provide"?*
2. *What does the addiction "prevent" from happening?*
3. *What good things does it "produce"?*
4. *What does it "protect" you or others from?*

Keep yourself aligned and LIST ONLY THE GOOD OR FUNNY THINGS.
Don't introduce split energy by finding the pros and the cons.
There is method to this madness!

....

....

....

....

....

....

....

....

....

We all have addictions in some form, an addiction to breathing is one of them (I saw you smile), and it serves NO PURPOSE to feel bad about any of them. Feeling bad is not a solid motivating factor to change; it's that negative judgement that keeps our energy stuck in the first place.

You only need to ask yourself, "How is feeling bad about this working out for me?"

1. **If you would like to change an addictive habit, GIVE UP the guilt, remorse and shame first and TAKE UP something that feels so much better instead. It really can be that easy.**

2. **Then stop identifying yourself as the addiction. Stop saying, MY cancer, MY bad habits, MY problems. Put some distance between you and it. Instead say things like, this cancer, that bad habit, those problems. It isn't YOU. It never was YOU. It's just energy that has momentum and now you can start to slow it down.**

The task isn't to try and get rid of an addiction; that keeps our attention on the past; the key is to find something more life enhancing to be addicted to NOW instead. You've already done the hard work by identifying what it is you want to let go. So stop talking about it, stop feeling bad about it, stop justifying why you do it, stop trying to get others to indulge in it, stop hiding it, stop lying to yourself about it, stop silently criticizing yourself because of it, stop dreading the (possible) consequences because of it, stop thinking you're alone in this, stop doubting your ability to get over it, stop saying you can't do it, stop joking about it and stop assuming you're a failure because you haven't yet found a way to master it!

Have you ever allowed yourself to FULLY ENJOY this addiction all the way through, without splitting your energy, without feeling guilty, without being ashamed, without assuming you should be remorseful, without worrying what society says about it, without being concerned about how

*others feel about it, without fighting the mere suggestion of letting
yourself feel really good about it, without blaming someone or
something else for it, without fear of dying from it, without thinking
you're wrong, or bad, or flawed or broken in some way?*

B – R – E – A – T – H – E

What Would You Like To Become Addicted To Now?

I'd like to be addicted to making peace with where I'm at.
I'd like to be addicted to going easier on myself (and everyone else).
I'd like to be addicted to getting more massages, going for walks,
sitting in solitude for a while.
I'd like to be addicted to remembering the silly things.
I'd like to be addicted to spending time with animals.
I'd like to be addicted to imagining positive outcomes
I'd like to be addicted to speaking well of myself and others.
I'd like to be addicted to drinking more water.
I'd like to be addicted to going out in nature.
I'd like to be addicted to taking extra deep breaths in the fresh air.
I'd like to be addicted to doing really adventurous stuff.
I'd like to be addicted to living fully.
I'd like to be addicted to feeling alive.
I'd like to be addicted to allowing my creativity to flow.
I'd like to be addicted to spreading good news.
I'd like to be addicted to paying compliments.
I'd like to be addicted to appreciating what I already have.
I'd like to be addicted to making other people laugh.
I'd like to be addicted to having much more fun.
I'd like to be addicted to being who I really am.
I'd like to be addicted to loving myself anyway.
I'd like to be addicted to being insatiably happy.
I'd like to be addicted to joy.

The Spiritual 12 Step Program

This useful process is based on the teachings of Abraham-Hicks™ and has been purposefully rewritten and summarized from a workshop recording found freely on YouTube. Others have found it to be incredibly freeing, soothing and liberating. I think you will too.

1. Sometimes I feel powerless over this behaviour, and I'm looking forward to getting a handle on it.

2. I know that everything I want is in a much brighter place than where I've been and that my Inner Being/Source Energy/God is forever calling me towards the light. It's good for me to know that.

3. Since the life I've lived has got me to this place, I'm deciding that this is the best place to start anew. I make peace with my past and allow it to stay where it is and know that it provides a firm footing to know what I don't want and allows me to choose even more strongly, what I DO want for my life instead.

4. Life has caused me to know what I don't want, which lets me know clearly what I DO WANT. I'm now going to give my undivided attention towards WHAT I DO WANT! The moral inventory that I choose to see is that I AM MAGNIFICENT.

5. When I admit that I'm a bad person or that I've done a terrible thing — I feel bad. That negative emotion lets me know that I'm looking at myself in a way that my Inner Being/Source Energy/God does not do. The more I admit my wrongdoings, the more disconnected I become. I've decided to stop doing that and focus on the things that I AM DOING WELL instead.

6. I now understand that what I call God pays no attention to my defects and has only ever been seeing me as the perfect being that I AM. I've decided to do that too and see not only myself, but everyone else as the magnificent beings we ALL are.

7. I can't ask God to remove my shortcomings as God has never seen me as less than who I really am. As God doesn't pay attention to the negatives either, I've decided to now release my awareness of them as well and become much MORE aware of my positive aspects instead.

8. When I talk about the things I did in my PAST that were disappointing or harmful to others, I feel terrible, and I use that as my PRESENT excuse to hold myself apart from who I have already become. All of us will benefit so much more by focusing on the brightness of the FUTURE that we wish to see unfolding before us instead.

9. As much as it is nice to please others, I'm joyful in my knowledge that we all create our own reality. I will bring myself into alignment with my own Inner Being/Source Energy/God as best I can, but today I set everyone else free to create their own reality too and no longer need them to behave in any particular way so I can feel good.

10. Now I'm really flowing and I'm beginning to see myself the way my Inner Being/Source Energy/God knows me to be and I don't need to give attention to anything that is less than who I am becoming. I let go the past. I let go this last moment, I let go anything that is not who I intend to be and move gently towards the future I dream of creating.

11. I use meditation (to quieten my mind) and prayers of appreciation for what I've already been given, to gain a more conscious connection with my Inner Being/Source Energy/God as I understand it to be.

12. There were things in my life that I didn't know how to handle and I found temporary relief from the discomfort by using a substance to soothe the discord between me and my Inner Being/Source Energy/God. Now I know that I can get longer lasting relief by thinking about, talking about and focusing on things that make me feel better, that make me feel whole, that cause me to know the magnificent person I am inside and align me more with my Inner Being/Source Energy/God. My example shows other people the POWER of giving complete attention to getting emotional relief first, to what makes them feel better, to what causes them to know fully their own magnificence and come into closer alignment with their Inner Being/Source Energy/God too.

On the opposite side
of the darkest problem
is the most
BRILLIANT SOLUTION

Line up with that!

EMPOWERING PROCESS #17
To Change an Old Habit

"The best way to let go of something I don't want,
is to hold onto something that I do!" - ER

When I want to change an old habit, I don't say, "no, I'm not doing that anymore" to whatever I think the problem was. That just keeps my attention on the issue.

Instead, I practice saying "yes" to something new:

- ✓ I'm saying yes to a new way of thinking
- ✓ I'm saying yes to starting again
- ✓ I'm saying yes to giving myself a break
- ✓ I'm saying yes to lightening up a little
- ✓ I'm saying yes to making peace with where I'm at
- ✓ I'm saying yes to telling happier stories
- ✓ I'm saying yes to doing things different
- ✓ I'm saying yes to changing my posture
- ✓ I'm saying yes to finding relief
- ✓ I'm saying yes to moving my body
- ✓ I'm saying yes to quietening my mind occasionally
- ✓ I'm saying yes to taking more naps
- ✓ I'm saying yes to looking forward
- ✓ I'm saying yes to imagining positive outcomes
- ✓ I'm saying yes to improved health
- ✓ I'm saying yes to getting more massages
- ✓ I'm saying yes to noticing how I feel

- ✓ I'm saying yes to deciding where I want to go
- ✓ I'm saying yes to waiting for inspiration
- ✓ I'm saying yes to a higher quality of life
- ✓ I'm saying yes to remembering the good times
- ✓ I'm saying yes to talking about my success
- ✓ I'm saying yes to having more fun
- ✓ I'm saying yes to laughing out loud
- ✓ I'm saying yes to freedom
- ✓ I'm saying yes to turning myself on
- ✓ I'm saying yes to knowing real pleasure
- ✓ I'm saying yes to breathing even deeper
- ✓ I'm saying yes to feeling so much better
- ✓ I'm saying yes to opening my heart
- ✓ I'm saying yes to being more focused
- ✓ I'm saying yes to treating myself well
- ✓ I'm saying yes to accepting how far I've come
- ✓ I'm saying yes to liking who I am again
- ✓ I'm saying yes to love

What are you saying yes to?

....

....

....

....

....

EMPOWERING PROCESS #18
To Guarantee Instant Success

*"One of the Keys to Success is
to keep choosing the same thing!" – ER*

Momentum is powerful. It's the fuel of creation There are two basics ways to make decisions.

1. Wait until something happens and then make a decision, OR
2. Make a decision and line up with it.

But here's the way to make it work without introducing resistance.

Start with something general like, love, laughter, fun, freedom, peace, passion. I choose it again and again and again, and then allow it to evolve naturally. It makes no difference if I'm working or playing, I do whatever it takes to feel good right now! And I keep choosing it again and again and again.

I won't start work until I feel good, I won't get into a long conversation until I feel good, I won't attend a meeting until I feel good, I won't make a phone call until I feel good, I won't even TAKE a phone call until I feel good. The quality of every interaction I have throughout my day is guaranteed to be a success because I already feel good before I've begun. I don't leave anything to chance.

MOST PEOPLE WAIT UNTIL SOMETHING GOOD HAPPENS before they remember the phenomenal benefits of connecting to the "life force" that moves our energy naturally in a positive direction, but conscious creators "intend" to deepen their connection by deliberately focusing on any subject that makes them feel better than where they currently are.

ANY TIME YOU FEEL POSITIVE EMOTION (happy, blissful, content, passionate, energised, loving etc.) you are naturally aligned with your divine nature. Problems are solved quickly, the right words come easily, creativity is maximised, questions are answered clearly, confusion is replaced with clarity, disease is softened, peace is found, relief is instant, work is done effortlessly, passion bursts forth from within, inspiration is received, love is felt purely and life-force is infused throughout your entire body!

> *"My goal is to feel as good as I can in each moment just by choosing it again and again and again, and then let the universe show me where I intended to go all along, and it always turns out better than I imagined." – ER*

EMPOWERING PROCESS #19
To Get Organised

THE GAME: Here's how to sort out the to-do list so more stuff actually gets done - easily.

Get a piece of paper and make a line down the centre. On the left side, write "Things I Absolutely Must Do" Or "Things That I Am Happy to Do". On the other side put everything else and title it "Things I AM Giving the Universe to Do".

Then notice how much weight is taken off your shoulders. Woooosh ... some more resistance just lifted. How good does it feel to be a little bit lighter?

(Credit to Abraham-Hicks™ for this leading edge, extremely effective and empowering process).

~ Notes ~

EMPOWERING PROCESS #20
To Feel Better About Anything

7 Ways to Change Focus and Feel Better Quickly

I don't have to change my circumstances, I just decide how significant I want them to be, in the whole scheme of my life ~ ER

INTRODUCTION: This simple process has the potential to move you from despair, worry, doubt, fear or any number of negative emotions into a better feeling place, so you can think more clearly and most importantly, be inspired to the actions, solutions and answers that are just right for you.

The best use of our time isn't in running around trying to change circumstances, change other people or even to change a condition in our physical body – the best use of our time is to shift our emotional state first! Don't underestimate the power of these 7 simple ways. Reading the words alone will raise your vibration.

If you're already feeling high and happy – there's probably no need to go any further with this particular process, it's not really designed for you right now. However, you are welcome to come back any time you're feeling a bit down and would like to soothe yourself and uplift your spirits. Better still, why not write your own guide that fits your unique personality? Write the steps you personally take to relax and let your emotions move back naturally, to their most regular state.

But, if you are feeling a bit flat in this moment and could use a lift, relax as much as you can and read on ...

THE FIRST WAY: Make Peace with How I'm Feeling

Don't expect or even try to feel loving, grateful and appreciative immediately. If I'm upset, depressed, afraid, angry, feeling powerless, vengeful or anything else in between I'm not even close to those more pleasant emotions. It's better to allow myself to experience the anger, to feel the distress, to move through the turmoil until I'm REALLY READY to let it go.

When I am ready to make a shift, I make peace by not pushing against whatever has happened and allow the momentum of negative energy to slow down naturally. And it will, just like it's done countless times before.

THE SECOND WAY: Slow Down

Slow the energy down! It's all going to be OK. Hope to feel better soon.

Sometimes "hope" is the best feeling I can find for now. I'm simply aiming to feel a little better ... not striving for a quantum leap.

Hope is good.

Hope for improvement.

Hope to be given a sign that I've turned the corner and will be able to see the light, get the solution, receive the answer, feel the peace, really soon.

THE THIRD WAY: Find Relief

Find relief in any way I can, without judgment about how I do it. When I get relief I breathe deeper, I relax more and I make better choices.

Relief.

Relief.

Relief.

Relief.

Relief.

Just saying the word a few times helps me to feel better. If I write them down on a piece of paper, that helps to settle me too.

THE FOURTH WAY: Just Make One Decision

The only decision I want to make right now, is that I won't make any OTHER decisions until I'm feeling more stable. My best decisions are always made when I'm feeling empowered, feeling aligned and feeling much better than I am right now.

And that's OK. I've felt good before. I'll feel good again really soon.

THE FIFTH WAY: Stop Talking

Stop talking about the specific details of whatever's happened and be more general about it.

Remind myself how things have worked out before.

If I've been talking for a while and haven't yet found a better feeling attitude, silence usually soothes and settles the fast moving energy and calms my mood, until I regain my centre.

THE SIXTH WAY: Quieten My Mind

Meditate, go for a walk, sleep or do anything else to quieten my mind and vibrate in harmony with who I truly am, when I'm feeling my best.

THE SEVENTH WAY: Distract Myself Completely

Get off the subject. Stop trying to work on the problem ... breathe the fresh air ... drink more water ... relax my shoulders ... and allow the solution to be inspired. Watch a comedy, dance like a lunatic, move my body around, play in the park, go to the beach, take a bath, have a cold shower, light a candle, look up at the stars, keep my head held high, change my clothes, change my body posture, change my focus, bask in the sunshine, pat a cat.

Once I find that relief, I begin to lighten up, I allow better things to come and the energy gently shifts ... naturally ... as it was always meant to be.

"It's natural to feel good!"

WHAT ARE YOU SEARCHING FOR?

Search for reasons to be happy, for opportunities to laugh. Feel for a sense of stability, signs saying you're on the right path.

Notice the many things there are close by, to be ever so thankful for. Acknowledge that you keep on breathing, without even needing to take score.

Look for beauty in nature, in animals and in the people all around. Find pleasure in the simple things as well as in the profound.

Remember how the earth keeps revolving without us giving a second thought. Realize waterfalls, rivers and oceans, no one ever went out and bought.

Look for proof life is working out for you, and know you'll always want something more. The fact that things are going well, is the only evidence you need search for. - ER Dec 2017

EMPOWERING PROCESS #21
To Be an Influence in The World

YOUR TASK IF YOU CHOOSE TO ACCEPT IT: See each person in your life as already having achieved their wellness, already having created their wealth, already having attracted their ideal relationship, already living the life of their dreams. When you do this, not only will you feel better and attract similar conditions in your own life, but you'll be a powerful contributor to attracting those elements into their life too.

Remember how good it feels to be around someone who believes in you, who always sees the best in you, who knows you are capable, adaptable, worthy, valuable and whole – just as you are? Doesn't it help you feel better and make you shine a whole lot more too?

"Of course, it is a wonderful thing to help others, but you must do it from your position of strength and alignment, which means you MUST be in alignment with their success as you offer assistance, and not in alignment with their problem. When you feel an inspired eagerness to offer something because you want to participate in their happy, successful process, your attention to their success harmonizes with the point of view of your Source; and the infinite resources of the Universe are at your disposal. And that does help."
- Abraham-Hicks™

It serves no one to give added energy to the problems. Once you've identified what the problem is, flip as quickly as you can into being open to the solution. That keeps your energy flowing freely.

Problem >>> Solution. Problem >>> Solution. Problem >>> Solution.
Contrast is necessary for the expansion of the entire Universe.
What solutions would you like to be part of now?

....

....

....

....

....

....

....

....

....

....

EMPOWERING PROCESS #22
To Love Myself More

"I'm Focusing on the Best Parts of Me!"

Do you ever compare yourself to others? Are they more or less successful than you? Are they more or less happier than you? Do they have more or less luxury items that you? Are they enjoying better relationships that you? Do they go on more or less holidays than you?

If you feel superior when you've got something that's better than them, then you'll feel crushed when you don't. Comparing yourself to others is destructive in every case, so for this process, let's bring the focus back to you.

EMPOWERING PROCESS: Write down the answer to these 3 questions at the end of every day for the next 17 days. This simple process produces such a gentle but profound change in attitude, you might wonder why you haven't done it more often.

What am I happy about today? ....

What am I thankful for today? ....

What have I done well today? ....

~ Notes ~

EMPOWERING PROCESS #23
To Change My Attitude

Even the most uncomfortable and challenging situations get easier in the moment I change my attitude about them, re-claiming ownership of the powerfully attuned person I was born to be.

Each statement below gives a slightly different perspective to some common attitudes on health, wealth, relationships and happiness. Just reading them will make you think about what your attitudes and beliefs actually are, and bring them to more conscious awareness.

These attitudes aren't necessarily something I suggest you adopt, but by the end of this section you will be much clearer about how you might change some of your own, or it will make you realize you're perfectly happy just the way you are. Either way, you win!

I DIDN'T GET BETTER HEALTH BY SEARCHING FOR THE NEXT MIRACLE CURE ... I got better healthy by relaxing my way there, and by becoming someone who chooses to remember my spiritual well-being, notices my emotional state and tends lovingly to my mental focus, no matter what might have manifested physically.

I DIDN'T GET INCREASED WEALTH BY WAITING FOR THE RIGHT NUMBERS TO BE DRAWN ... I got increased wealth by playing and enjoying my way there, and by becoming someone who appreciates ALL that I have in my life right now and excitedly anticipates even more in the future.

I DIDN'T FIND SUCCESS BY LOOKING FOR IT … I became successful by being true to my own desires and letting the good things in life find me.

I DIDN'T GET INTO A GREAT RELATIONSHIP BY HOPING THE RIGHT PERSON WOULD SHOW UP … I got into a great relationship by experiencing and practicing my way there and by becoming the sort of person who appreciates the growth and expansion that ALL relationships offer.

I DON'T GET WHAT I WANT BY FIGHTING FOR IT … I stay silent, stay positive, stay aligned and allow it to manifest in its own way, in its own time and with results that amaze even me. Fighting is fraught with resistance. Allowing, trusting and believing is an indication I am in pure alignment with everything I've ever wished for.

I DON'T HAVE A GREAT LIFE BECAUSE EVERYTHING GOES WELL … I just accept that life has its ups and downs and choose to find creative ways to turn the 'shit' into valuable fertilizer anyway.

I DIDN'T FIND MY PLACE IN THE WORLD BY TAKING THE ADVICE OF OTHERS … I let the right way unfold naturally by noticing what brings me relief, what feels so much better, what makes me really happy, what fills me with passion, what energizes me to action, what leads me to joy, what lights up my life and then by moving with gentle persistence towards more of it.

I DON'T GET THROUGH MY PROBLEMS BY WORKING ON THEM … I spend time appreciating what's already going well in my life and allow what isn't, to transform gently into solutions.

I DIDN'T GAIN RESPECT BY COMMANDING IT … respect came naturally when instead of speaking my mind, I speak from the heart!

I DON'T HAVE A RICH LIFE BECAUSE I HANG ON TO THE MONEY
I'VE EARNED ... Money flows in and out, in and out like the air that
I breathe, and there's always more where that came from.

I once thought that money would make me happy; that if I was smart
enough, if I found the best investments, if I worked really hard, I'd be
able to live the good life! But then I discovered, when I did the things
that felt good to me it didn't matter if I made money out of them or
not! I was already living the good life, and opportunities, ideas and
more money than I ever needed, just came as a result!

When I had a poorer life, I thought I needed to get everything cheap,
I wouldn't pay full price and knew things were going to be tough.
Now my life is incredibly rich; I let myself dream about whatever
tickles my fancy, I declare "*I can have anything my heart desires*" and
I know that the ways, the means will always be inspired.

What changed to move me from poorer to richer? ... My attitude!
"*I can have it, just because I want it - period!*"

I DON'T GET WHAT I WANT BY IMPLEMENTING AN ACTION PLAN ...
I take time to attune my thoughts, my attitudes, my words, and my
vibration, into believing it's already done, and when I feel good about
that, the right action is divinely inspired with no agenda in mind.

The universe always gives me what I ask for, but it doesn't just hear
my words, think my thoughts or know my action ... it feels my
emotional vibration and gives me exactly what I'm putting out.

I DIDN'T GET HAPPY BY EXPECTING OTHER PEOPLE TO CHANGE ...
I got happy by changing my own thoughts, words and actions and
by bringing them into harmony with who I know inside we all really
are ... magnificent souls all doing the very best we can in each
blessed moment.

I DON'T HAVE A GREAT NIGHT OUT BECAUSE I'VE CHOSEN THE RIGHT ENVIRONMENT, THE RIGHT FRIENDS AND THE RIGHT CLOTHES ... I enjoy myself immensely just by focusing on the best parts of life, no matter where I am, who I'm with and how I look.

I DON'T NEED TO MAKE THINGS HAPPEN ... Life gets so much easier every time I STOP trying to "make" something happen and start focusing on what I WANT to experience and why I want it. There's often a better road that takes me towards my desires and when I trust it will be shown to me, the way is always paved so well I stand back in awe.

MY HEART ... It isn't breaking, it's expanding.

What new attitudes are you inspired to adopt now?

....

....

....

....

....

....

EMPOWERING PROCESS #24
To Help Anyone Feel Better

"Focus on something that makes your soul come alive, then you won't need to fix or change anything at all. Any issues will cease to exist in those moments. And as one moment expands to more, one day you realize, you didn't even need to look for a solution at all, the solution found you." – ER

Do your best to stop focusing on the problem. That just makes it bigger. Even when you look for a solution to a problem it's still activating the energy of the problem.

So I like to do something that changes the energy entirely. Once I start to feel better I can really throw my heart and soul into the day and never look back. If I need a helping hand to get there, I do this simple process and talk about what I'd rather do instead.

- ❖ I'D RATHER TRUST THE PROCESS … than doubt a favourable outcome.
- ❖ I'D RATHER EXPECT THE BEST … than plan for the worst.
- ❖ I'D RATHER RELAX … than worry.
- ❖ I'D RATHER FIND HAPPINESS NOW … than wait for things to change.
- ❖ I'D RATHER DEMONSTRATE HOW I LIKE TO BE … than give advice on what someone else should do.
- ❖ I'D RATHER EAT FOR PLEASURE … than starve my soul.
- ❖ I'D RATHER FEEL BEAUTIFUL ON THE INSIDE … than care about how others think I look on the outside.

- ❖ I'D RATHER RETREAT IN SILENCE … than act in anger.
- ❖ I'D RATHER OPEN MY HEART … than close my mind.
- ❖ I'D RATHER BELIEVE EVERYONE HAS GOOD INTENTIONS … than question their motives.
- ❖ I'D RATHER CHANGE MY ATTITUDE … than change the world.
- ❖ I'D RATHER FIND PEACE INSIDE … than fight to prove I'm right.
- ❖ I'D RATHER LOVE.

What would you rather do?

....

....

....

....

....

....

....

....

....

....

EMPOWERING PROCESS #25
To Reclaim My Power

THE TASK: Develop your own Power Statements that remind you of *Who You Really Are* and *What You Really Want*, especially when you need it the most.

The following empowering phrase brings me back to centre quickly if I'm tempted to reach for comfort food, work too much, get involved in a conversation that's heading for disaster or if I'm asked to do something I'd just rather not do.

My personal Power Statement of What I Really Want is:

> *"I want to look good.*
> *I want to FEEL good.*
> *I want to treat myself good."*

THE POWER OF WOMAN: This next empowering phrase was written as a way to bring myself into even closer alignment first thing in the morning. I know people who print it, laminate it and put it in the back of the bathroom door and *"declare"* it while they're showering. For this purpose we call it *"The Shower of Power"*. A well-known global women's network also uses it as their Facebook page banner, I've recording myself speaking it to play on my iPod when I'm out walking and I often use it as my desktop wallpaper too. Say it with power and feeling for the next 17 days and see what happens.

My Power Statement of Who I Really Am is:

I am Loving, I am Beautiful, I am Joyful, I am Kind,
I am Expansive, I am Radiant, I have Peace and Clarity of Mind.

I am Magnetic, I am Creative, I am Receptive, I am Inspiring, I am
Original, I am Abundant, I am Graceful, I am Amazing.

I am Magnificent, I am Protected, I am Served and I'm Adored, I am
Treasured, I am Admired and I am Supported even more.

I am Grateful, I am Magical, I am Power, I am Light,
I am Appreciative, I am Valuable, I am Wisdom, I have Insight.

I am Passion and Inspiration, and Content I love to BE.
I am in the Flow, I am Wealthy, I am Wise, I am ME!

I am Present, I am Fulfilled, I am Perfectly Complete,
My Emotions are Empowering, from the Heart I like to Speak.

My Body, Mind and Spirit are in Total Harmony.
I am Blissful, I am Ecstatic, I am Whole, I am FREE.

THE POWER OF MAN: After sharing The Power of Woman poster publicly, men asked if they too could have one specifically for them. The following statements were compiled after researching the personal phrases that some of the men I admire the most use to boost their passion, power, and charisma.

YES, I live with passion
I am success
I am power and perseverance
I am invincible
I am STRONG

I take action
I am focused
I am a lover and a warrior
I face challenges with courage and determination
I am respected

I cherish and adore my woman
I love as if there are no others
Her happiness means the world to me
My life has meaning, vision and purpose
I build bigger and better and I am incredible
I am creative and I can solve ANYTHING

I am of service, I add massive value
I am proud and I am significant
I am a protector
I am a force for good
I AM a LEADER

I am healthy and wealthy
I live with honour and integrity
I am dependable and provide solid support
I am responsible
I am a WINNER
I am God

THE POWER OF LOVE: These next words were inspired from a
very powerful Tony Robbins workshop, that brought an estranged
husband and wife back together again after years of discomfort and
conflict. While these aren't necessarily words that I would personally
use, I showed them to a special man in my life and he was so moved,
he sent through a beautiful recording of himself very passionately
declaring them to me.

Your needs are my needs
I love you ... I'm here for you
I love you no matter what you do or say
Nothing will ever take my love away
I want for you what YOU want for you
For YOU, I will do anything, ANYTHING!

You are home to me
I love you ... Come home to my heart
There's no place like YOU

There's no force on EARTH like you
There's no LOVE like YOU
I worship you ... I ADORE you

I love you ... I NEED you ... I will NEVER settle without you
I own your soul ... I will take care of your soul
I am always here for you
I will never leave you
I will take care of you forever
You and you alone I worship

I adore you ... I worship you ... I LOVE you
My heart is at home with you
There's no place like HOME
There's no PLACE like home
There's NO place like home!
You are my home ... YOU are my love ... YOU are my destiny!

◉ SIDE NOTE: The power of any of these statements is not contained in the words; it's contained in HOW the words move energy in you!

What are your Power Statements?

....

....

....

....

....

EMPOWERING PROCESS #26
To Make My Dreams Come True

*"Instead of being a deliberate creator,
be a deliberate receiver!"*

Choose a big dream. Any dream will do. Choose just one and imagine it for a few moments. Then decide WHO you would need to become to have it, to create it, to manifest it, to be it, to live it.

Choosing an identity first is far more powerful than trying to take action to make a dream come true, and it's so much more fun too.

QUESTION: WHO do I need to become to live this dream?

....

....

....

....

....

....

~ Notes ~

EMPOWERING PROCESS #27
To Calm Down

B-R-E-A-T-H-E

"Just breathe your way to peace.
It's the most natural thing in the world."

EMPOWERING PROCESS #28
To Make Better Choices

"One of the best things you can do is to decide
you're worth more and Raise Your Standards!"

Whatever you are thinking, saying and doing NOW is a reflection of your past choices. Never let anything stand in your way of making a better choice. Don't let what's happening INSIDE you stand in your way - and don't let what's happening OUTSIDE you stand in your way. Because *you* have the power to make a brand new decision *now* if you don't like something that's going on in your life.

Some people might think that they can't produce better results - and if YOU think that too, then you're right. Your mind accepts everything you tell it. But, let's just try these questions:

1. What have you allowed to happen in your life that you didn't STOP from happening (sometimes known as enabling)?

2. Have you allowed dis-empowering thoughts about yourself or others to enter into your mind (sometimes known as negative thinking)?

3. Have you allowed other people to disturb you from believing you can reach a big dream (sometimes known as thwarted intention)?

4. Have you allowed yourself to speak disrespectfully of others (sometimes known as "tall poppy syndrome" or gossip)?

5. Have you allowed yourself to regularly indulge in things that you clearly feel guilty or ashamed about (sometimes known as addictions)?

What things have you allowed into your life that is simply NOT GOOD ENOUGH FOR YOU anymore?

I'd like to let go:

....

....

....

I'd like to choose these things instead:

....

....

....

....

....

....

....

....

EMPOWERING PROCESS #29
To Start My Day Off Well

PART 1

IF I COULD HAVE IT All MY WAY ~~~~~~~~~~~~~~~~~~~~~~
Imagine that!

THE PROCESS: Imagine having things the way YOU want them as if it's not only possible – but well and truly done! Dart into a thought and dart out again before you start adding resistance to the story. Enjoy 68 seconds or more of pure fantasy, and start your day in a magical way.

PART 2

PRAYER TO MY INNER BEING (Adapted from the Teachings of Abraham-Hicks™)

Inner-Being. I'm wanting this day to begin with the acknowledgement of how perfect I am, how pure I am, how worthy I am, how wondrous I am, how special I am, how valued I am, how prosperous I am, how whole I am.

Give me the feeling of that just for a moment, just a glimpse, just a little feeling.

I got it. Thank you.

~ Notes ~

EMPOWERING PROCESS #30
To Transform A Relationship

Want A Quick Way To Transform A Relationship?

It's natural for us to make up meanings for things that occur and reasons for why we think other people do what they do. Each person makes up their own meanings in an attempt to make sense of their perspective on life. No two people will have the same set of meanings for every topic; it really is an individual thing.

Let's say someone just spoke angrily to you. It could mean:

1. They don't like you;
2. You've done something to provoke them;
3. They are having bad day;
4. You have attracted their anger because you're a bad person;
5. They thought you deserved to be yelled at;
6. You are a good person and they are in the wrong;
7. They are trying to help you hear something important;
8. They feel comfortable enough to be themselves around you;
9. OR, it is what it is and you don't need to attach any meaning to it at all.

WHAT IF …
there's a good reason this person
is behaving like this?

From these examples, can you see the multitude of options we have to choose from for why people are behaving the way they are? Of course, sometimes our options seem a little limited, because we've built up such a strong "*perception*" about life, that it's difficult to imagine there might be other, more supportive ways we could see the same situation.

But that doesn't mean you "tolerate" their behaviour either. Tolerating isn't a positive action, it's a defeatist attitude. Put your own life jacket on first, and when you're stable then you can add value to others.

So I'm about to give you an empowering meaning that has the potential to make everything that's happened in past, present and future relationships, look very different. It might be a stretch, but if you've never done it before, I promise you it's worth contemplating, even if it's just for a day.

"Imagine that everything the other person says or does is because they love you!"

END NOTE: It doesn't even matter if you "believe" it's true or not. Just contemplate it for a while. Doesn't it make you feel better when you think about it? That's the purpose and the benefit right there.

EMPOWERING PROCESS #31
To Move On From A Relationship

When we really want to let go of something, it's much more sustainable if we find something to HOLD ON TO as well.

- ❖ If we want to let go a few kilos – hold on to getting fitter or stronger.
- ❖ If we want to let go something that's been a struggle – hold on to ease or peace.
- ❖ If we want to let go negative thoughts – hold on to quietening the mind for a while.
- ❖ If we want to let go a relationship – well, just read the poem below ...

Don't just try to let go, say hello, to something improved, something more than before, something shiny and new, because that's what the Universe is lining up for you!

Letting go, is giving your attention to the past.
Focusing forward ensures the transformation will last!
Talk endlessly about what you really want now,
think about "why", but, forget the "how".

Our task is to ask,
then trust we'll be inspired,
to the actions that harmonize,
with our most important core desires.

We were all born with guidance;
knowing when something feels right,
if it's been more like a struggle,
you're ready to give up the fight.

What causes the suffering is when you close down your heart,
if you've been holding someone at fault, don't tear yourself apart …
… you see your own inner being loves this person just as they be,
and that's the conflict right there, if you disagree.

Relationships are eternal, they weren't meant to end,
in fact, we really can't break them, we can only pretend,
that the other has wronged us in ways unforgivable,
set yourself free; do those things again that made life together,
so joyously liveable.

Remember the Love you happily gave right at the start?
That was really a gift to yourself … so just re-open your heart!

~ ~ ~

END NOTE: Too often we get bogged down in the "who did what to who" story. Keep going for the dream!

It isn't the other person we need to let go of, it isn't the "*attachment*" we need to let go of, it isn't the situation we need to let go of, we just need to keep holding on to our DREAM. Letting go assumes that someone can hold us back. Only we can do that.

Just keep going for the dream.
Keep GOING for the dream.
KEEP GOING FOR THE DREAM.

They'll either come along for the ride or someone else will jump on board. Go for your DREAM and lead yourself, back into the light!

EMPOWERING PROCESS #32
To Start All Over Again

If we want, we can start all over again at the beginning of each new day. We don't have to wait until a tragedy strikes to have a clean, new and fresh perspective on life. This process works to start again on a topic that has you firmly in its grasp too.

HERE'S THE EMPOWERING SUGGESTION: Find the blessings in everything that happens and if you can't find them, make them up. Life is created largely through the stories we tell, so you might as well make them good ones.

THE PROCESS: Think about the story you've been telling about your health, your relationship, your work, your financial situation, your home, your Government or something else that's been happening in the world.

Is telling that old story making anything better?

If not, make a decision to start writing a new one and uplift your own spirits and the spirits of the people around you too.

A LITTLE GIFT: There's a special treat on the next page just for you. It's a place where you can write the title of your new story with space to add your name as well. Would this be a good time to give yourself a new name? Something that moves powerful positive energy in you! This process works on subtle, deep levels. Trust it!

EMPOWERING PROCESS #33
To Catch Up with My Dreams

"We want you to train yourself into UNREALISTIC THOUGHTS.
We want you to stop all of this realism you've got going on.
We want you to stop facing reality and start creating reality, because
it will change in the moment that your vibration changes." -
Abraham-Hicks™

For those who find traditional goal setting boring and ineffective, "Dream Catching" is a great new approach. It was the process I used to manifest the most wonderful relationship I've ever had and is the topic of a whole other book. But you can't stuff it up, so I wanted to give you the foundation of it here because it's so much fun – and it works way better than anything I've ever done!

Take yourself to a place, either an actual location or somewhere special in your mind, where your dreams have already been achieved. Feel what that feels like until you are in a state of bliss; like the daydreaming you did when you were a child.

Pretend you are walking towards your dreams and catching them, meeting up with them, bringing them to life.

When you're in that day-dreamy state, allow a really ridiculous, whimsical, silly or insanely huge idea to enter your mind, possibly something you dreamed about when you were younger. Catch it and hold it! Take it with you and watch what happens next.

Too many times, we don't choose the right dreams to focus on.

DREAM BIG!

Small ones can make us feel like failures if we don't achieve them and they're boring too. With big ones you have nothing to lose, and new energy, new life, new impulses, new passions and new ideas are created because of them.

EMPOWERING PROCESS #34
To Get Back To Centre Quickly

*"If I want something to change, changing my vibration
is the first, most powerful action I can ever take.
Any further action is inspired from there.
Life is often easier than we think!" – ER*

What do you do when something throws you out of your happy-place?

Do you have a strategy to calm yourself down and get back to centre, like taking a few deep breaths, reaching for comfort food, going for a walk, pouring a drink, laughing out loud, lighting a cigarette or meditating?

Habits are often picked up unconsciously as a mechanism to restore calm, especially if we've felt out of control of the situation that shifted our state in that downwards direction in the first place. The more aware you become of your emotions and the habits you've adopted to try and soothe them in the past, the more they can work for you.

Most of the empowering processes listed in this book, are strategies to change your emotional state first, connecting you more fully to spirit, which then attracts better thoughts, improved words and inspired actions.

But sometimes, the ability to change something physically, makes changing your emotions easier too, especially if you catch the first negative thought or feeling pretty quickly. So the next time something happens that throws you out of that happy-place, say ah ha, now I've got some new strategies to consider.

CHANGE YOUR BODY POSTURE ... Hold your head up, align your spine, stand straight, maybe go for a walk, a run or put on some music and dance but whatever you do, do something that moves you from where you were when the negative thoughts and emotions started happening.

CHANGE YOUR FOCUS ... I once thought that to feel better about something, I needed to change it. Then I realised I didn't need to change *it* at all, I just needed to change what I was *focusing* my attention on. So tonight while I was out walking, I found the brightest light in the distance, maintained my gaze on it and walked towards it. Pretty soon I was laughing again, wondering what I was worried about in the first place. You could choose all sorts of things to focus on, like a flickering flame, sparkles on the water or anything that takes your fancy. The purpose of doing something like this is to slow the momentum of your thoughts enough, that you can then easily turn the energy around.

CHANGE YOUR CLOTHES ... Yes, that works too. You probably know how good it feels to get out of your clothes after you come home from work and slip into something comfortable. Now you can change your clothes when you've been feeling like crap and change how you're feeling as well. Maybe shoes is your thing, or sunglasses or a super hero costume or sexy lingerie! No matter what it is, changing into something that makes us feel special, is often all we need to do.

CHANGE YOUR BELIEF ... Reality is over-rated and giving constant attention to something that's impossible to change is the biggest cause of more unhappiness, depression, stress and disease than anything else. Make a decision that feeling better right now is a priority and that you'll do whatever it takes to find relief. Go for relief. Aim for relief. Settle into relief.

CHANGE YOUR LOCATION … When we start feeling good more often, it gets to become more of our natural state. Energy flows effortlessly, we are more at ease, we seem to have more control over our focus and life runs relatively smoothly; that's why when our emotions shift in a downward direction, we feel it more than ever before. So next time you feel that shift in energy, notice what set it off then move from where you are to somewhere else. Movement is such a great strategy to naturally allow any resistance to release.

CHANGE YOUR PERSPECTIVE … I once thought that if I could change the world, it would be a better place to live, then I looked around and saw how incredibly beautiful it already is, and I thought about how nice other people are to me, and I talked about the wonderful aspects of it all, and then I suddenly realised, I'd already made it better by changing my perspective, I'd already made a difference by soothing myself into feeling better too, and then I knew, that the only thing that needed to change was me, it was all good and I was right where I needed to be!

CHANGE THE STORY … Now this is where whimsy, fun, playfulness and magic really come in handy. Take the story you've been telling in your mind and imagine it ending with a really surprising twist, maybe superman came and saved the day, maybe you're in a real life fairy-tale, maybe a magician sprinkled everything with magic dust and all sorts of things that had been bothering you changed completely. You will know if the new story is working for you by the way it makes you feel. If it feels good, take that piece and run with it. Telling it over and over making it more elaborate until the energy shifts completely and you feel like yourself again.

USE GOD/SPIRIT/EXPANDED SELF … When I'm troubled, I ask for help and I *expect* it to come. I often feel guidance at the back of my head and neck, as if I'm being gently shown the way. Some people close their eyes and see visions, some will be called to write, some hear messages, some receive an impulse, some connect to animals, some may be inspired to new song lyrics and others may be moved to dance. Guidance is always there for us in every moment of every day. It's easier to feel its presence when we're high and happy, but never-the-less, it's always there. Use it.

1. *ASK FOR WHAT YOU WANT TO BE SHOWN TO YOU*

2. *RELAX AND ALLOW THE ANSWER TO COME*

EMPOWERING PROCESS #35
To Thank The Universe

Part 1

Thank the Universe for all the good things you don't know about yet.
(Courtesy - Abraham-Hicks™)

....

....

....

To Thank The Universe
Part 2

I love money ... and I like how you keep showing me interesting, unique and different ways for money to flow.

I love my body ... and I adore how you keep my blood pumping, my heart beating, my cells regenerating, my hair growing, my eyes seeing, my muscles strengthening, my system thriving.

I love relationships ... and I really appreciate how you keep matching me with like-minded, funny, easy-going, gorgeous, happy, uplifting people.

I love intimacy ... and oh my goodness, I'm blown away by the intensely pleasurable sensations I get to experience in conscious communion with others.

I love animals ... and I'm incredibly happy to be blessed by their company, their beauty, their entertaining presence, their balancing energy, their unconditional acceptance.

I love food ... and wow, thank you for providing me with so much variety, so many textures, scintillating flavours, such deliciously enjoyable fuel.

I love this planet ... and I'm in awe of how you keep the sun rising, the rain falling, the plants growing, the soil replenishing, the rivers flowing, the flowers blooming, the birds singing and all of life constantly evolving.

I love clarity ... and I'm thoroughly delighted to be gifted daily infusions of Pure Energy, Creativity, Passion, Vision and Purpose.

I love to focus ... and I greatly appreciate how you keep guiding me to uplifting thoughts, new ideas and inspired actions, that are in harmony with my core Desires.

I love alignment ... and I really, really like how you keep bringing me evidence of how life works best, in comfortable, humorous and the most delightful ways.

Thank You. I Love You. I know I AM a Valued and Worthy part of YOU.

EMPOWERING PROCESS #36
To Release Resistance

"In the moment that it feels uncomfortable, the contrast has served its purpose, which is usually instantaneous! But humans milk it, for unknown reasons. We would put up with negative emotion not at all if we were standing in your physical shoes." - Abraham-Hicks™

HERE'S THE KEY TO RELEASING RESISTANCE

Let go the need for manifestation!!!

Yes, that's it! Let go the need for manifestation. Give it up! Let go of that piece of resistance. Turn in a different direction, lighten up, breathe deeply, relax your shoulders, release the tension, go with the flow, laugh out loud, trust the process, feel the love ... instant relief.

Let go contrast as quick as you can!

EMPOWERING PROCESS #37
To Be A Conscious Creator

"The Universe isn't blessing you or cursing you,
it's just reflecting back your dominant vibe.
Change the vibe - Change the condition!"

The power is in your hands!

Many of us were taught to ask GOD to give us what we want.
These days we have a better understanding that we ARE God, that
we perceive our own realities and attract the conditions we call our
life ... so when there's something you want that you don't yet have,
why not go directly to Source ... YOU!

"Behave as if YOU have the power to direct your life!"

I'm not suggesting that you *"pretend"* something that you don't
believe to be true. Pretending is fleeting. It only lasts as long as we
have our attention on the pre-tense of what it is we think we want.

With this experiment, I'm suggesting you *"Take Command"* of the
situation.

Here are some examples:

Instead of praying for a cure for cancer or some other disease …… (What's the opposite of cancer = health. What's the opposite of disease = ease) …… intend health and ease, live healthy and easily, be health-full and at ease.

Instead of wanting to lose weight …… (Ask yourself why you want to lose weight. Maybe it's because you want to look better) …… intend to look better, treat yourself better, live better, feel better, be better.

Instead of hoping to win the lottery …… (Ask yourself why you want that? Is it for the sense of freedom you'd feel with financial improvement?) …… intend financial improvement, live in ways that improve your financial situation, feel what it feels like to improve your financial situation, be financially free.

STOP praying for what you want from something outside yourself. You and I are Source. INTEND IT! COMMAND IT! CREATE IT! BE IT!

I Now Intend …………………………………………………………………………………………………….

………..

………..

I AM Now Creating ……………………………………………………………………………………………

………..

………..

………..

EMPOWERING PROCESS #38
To Let Go And Trust The Process

"The more it feels like something needs to be fixed the more you need to let it go!" - Abraham-Hicks™

How do I let go resistance?

Stop doing what you keep on doing, stop thinking what you keep on thinking and stop talking about what you keep on talking about that keeps you feeling stuck right where you are.

Instead, think, say and do the things that make you feel relieved, that make you feel soothed, that make you feel free, that make you feel open and that make you feel truly alive!

Would you like to play "Letting Go" with me?

It's a game inspired by the teachings of Abraham, to help us release the resistant vibration that's been holding back the things we want, from coming to us easily.

HERE'S HOW IT WORKS:

1. Whether we are wanting more money, a house, a relationship, a health cure, a career change, or to fix a specific problem in our lives — we just LET IT GO for the next 30 days.

2. We trust that it's in our vortex, and we simply release the urgency for the condition to change right now. We do our best to let go of

that resistant topic — and LEAVE IT WITH THE UNIVERSE TO MANAGE for these next few weeks.

3. Rather than stressing about, focusing on, trying to find solutions for or strategizing about that particular thing — we decide to enjoy ourselves and BASK IN THE GOOD FEELING WE PREFER TO FEEL instead.

4. If we find ourselves thinking about that thing again — we are kind to ourselves, we just gently release it for now and PIVOT BACK TO AN EASY FEELING VIBE.

5. We acknowledge that WE ARE COMPLETELY FREE TO PICK IT UP AGAIN next month if we choose to do so — or not!

I play this game regularly, want to join in?

Send an email to fun@elizabethrichardson.info with the subject line "LETTING GO" if you'd like to play along. Tell me if there's something I can do to support you in having even more fun with this fabulous game. I'd love to hear from you.

Checking Your Progress

LET'S DO A QUICK CHECK TO FIND OUT WHERE YOU ARE RIGHT NOW AFTER READING THE BOOK AND/DOING THE PROCESSES.

On a scale of 1 – 10 (with 10 being the highest, the most, the best, the greatest) write down the answer to each of these next questions.

How relaxed and at ease am I feeling right now about:

1. My health.
2. My physical body.
3. My finances, sense of freedom and money.
4. My family and relationships.
5. My work, career or business.
6. My home, location and environment.
7. My contentment and satisfaction with the life I'm currently living.
8. My ability to be, do have and create more of what I want in the future.
9. My connection to Spirit/Source/God/Higher Self?

QUESTIONS: Checking back on your answers from the first section of the book called "Monitoring Your Progress", how does this compare to where you were when you started reading?

What area or areas of your life have improved?

What process or game worked really well for you?

What insights did you receive?

What things are you genuinely inspired to do now to release
resistance more often?

....

....

....

....

....

....

....

....

....

....

....

....

....

....

Thank You

Thank you for the goodness in front of us.
Thank you for the friends beside us.
Thank you for the roof that shelters us.
Thank you for the love circulating in, through and all around us.

Thank you for the passion that propels us.
Thank you for the joy that exudes from us.
Thank you for the peace that abides in us.
Thank you for the abundance that's gifted to us.

Thank you for the food that nourishes us.
Thank you for the choices that excite us.
Thank you for the air and water that sustains us.
Thank you for incredible bodies that continue to adapt in spite of us.

Thank you for thoughts that encourage us.
Thank you for words that soothe us.
Thank you for actions that value, cherish and acknowledge us.
Thank you for relationships which nurture, comfort and move us.

Thank you for the animals that balance us.
Thank you for the natural world that surrounds us.
Thank you for the people who really care about us.
Thank you for death which provides instant relief for us.

Thank you for the fun that explodes in us.
Thank you for the opportunities that are attracted to us.
Thank you for the desires that are strong in us.
Thank you for the creations that manifest because of us.

Thank you for beliefs that uplift us.
Thank you for our emotions that firmly guide us.
Thank you for the flow of Universal Energy that replenishes us.
Thank you for Infinite Intelligence that's inspired though us.

Thank you for the contrasting experiences that expand us.
Thank you for Divine Life that effortlessly breathes us.
Thank you for the Grace that showers over us.
Thank you for everything that's so readily available to restore us,
enhance us and truly empower us. – ER February 2017

###

Note from The Author

Thank you so much for sharing your time with me. If there's one problem I can help you release resistance on, get in touch and let me know. If you have received value from any of the empowering processes in this book, and don't keep it a secret; please take a moment to write a short review. It is greatly appreciated.

Elizabeth Richardson

Contact Details

Author: Elizabeth Richardson (ER)
Website: https://elizabethrichardson.info

Other Publications

https://amazon.com/author/elizabethrichardson

www.ingramcontent.com/pod-product-compliance
Lightning Source LLC
LaVergne TN
LVHW021505080426
835509LV00018B/2401